PLAY IT FOR LAUGHS

FIVE COMEDIES FOR THIRTY KIDS

BILL TORDOFF

HEINEMANN
SPOTLIGHTS

Heinemann Educational Books

Heinemann Educational Books Ltd
Halley Court, Jordan Hill, Oxford OX2 8EJ
OXFORD   LONDON   EDINBURGH
MADRID   PARIS   ATHENS   BOLOGNA
MELBOURNE   SYDNEY   AUCKLAND
IBADAN   NAIROBI   GABORONE   HARARE
SINGAPORE   TOKYO   PORTSMOUTH (NH)

91   92   93   94   95   14   13   12   11   10   9   8   7   6   5

ISBN 435 23900 7

Printed in England by Clays Ltd, St Ives plc

CONTENTS

Introduction v

The Assembly Show 7

Foul Play At Sunny Bay 27

The Best In The Book 57

The Class Struggle 79

Robby Nudd 107

INTRODUCTION

These plays were originally written for performance at Rodillian School, Leeds (formerly Rothwell Grammar School), where there is a long tradition of staging plays which aim to give as many pupils as possible the chance to enjoy the experience of putting on a show together. Looking for suitable plays to produce, I became increasingly frustrated as I searched through the local library. Most of the short plays had small casts, often of one sex, and many tried to be literary rather than dramatic. I decided that I would have to write the plays that I was looking for: lively plays with parts for everyone in a mixed class. Nearly every play in this collection has a nominal cast of 15 girls and 15 boys. (Inevitably, some parts are larger than others, but every one is a character with individual lines as well as choruses to join in.) Although these scripts were all written for performance they can, of course, be used for reading in class or as the basis of work in Drama.

NOTES FOR NOVICE DIRECTORS

Preparation

All these plays have been altered in the light of production since they were first written; if you want to change them in any way, feel free! For a start, unless you have exactly 15 actors of each sex you will want to increase or decrease the number of parts by sharing out the lines differently, and you will probably need to reallocate the parts between the sexes, changing names as appropriate.

Make sure that you work out moves and groupings of characters before you start to rehearse, even if you have to modify them later.

Acting

In large-cast plays such as these, few of the cast will be speaking at any given time. As director, you need constantly to remind your cast that acting consists not only of saying lines but in remaining in part throughout. (When not speaking, an actor will not go far wrong if he looks at whoever is speaking, his expression showing his reactions.) When individual lines are being spoken by members of a group, it helps to draw the audience's attention if an actor moves slightly as he starts to speak. And remember that a meaningful silence is often more effective than words.

Learning a part

Once the cast know how to say their lines and when to move, they can learn their parts. They need to learn to speak their lines clearly and with feeling, on cue and with the appropriate moves. (And point out that learning a part also includes learning lines or choruses spoken by a group.)

Later rehearsals

Throughout rehearsals, your actors need to speak as loudly as in performance. To this end, the director should conduct later rehearsals from the back of the room. Once scripts are down, rehearsals should begin to approximate to performance, using props and costumes. In plays of more than one scene, practise going straight from one scene to another, with scenery and props struck and set very quickly. If production is to go smoothly, it is vital that properties (or substitutes) are used in rehearsals. It needs constant practice both to remember lines and to cope with important props such as the teacher's keys in *The Class Struggle*, the bears in *Sunny Bay* and the gifts in *The Best In The Book*.

Above all, keep reminding yourself that it's all worthwhile; after the inevitable difficulties and frustrations of rehearsals, there are few feelings more pleasant than the elation (and relief!) when your cast take their final curtain-call.

B.T.

THE ASSEMBLY SHOW

CHARACTERS

MR BIG, *headmaster*
MR CRUNCHER, *boys' games*
MISS HARTY, *girls' games*
MISS FISH, *swimming coach*
MR SMOOTHLY, *indoor games*
REV. D. J. BRIGHTLY, *R.S. teacher*
MISS GROOVY, *young English teacher*
MRS ELDERBERRY, *senior mistress*
TEACHERS 1–9
COMPERE 1
COMPERE 2
COMMENTATOR
WEATHERMAN
READER 1
READER 2
J. POTWELL
TRACY FROGTHORPE
PUPILS 1–9

NON-SPEAKING

OLD-STYLE TEACHERS
ROLLER-SKATER
VICTIM
HOSTESS
KIM
PAT
SHARON
JANICE
JOANNE

(NOTE: Nearly all parts, except MR BIG, can be doubled)

NOTE ON STAGING

The two sets of seats, for pupils and staff, must be at a shallow angle so that all the cast are fully visible to the audience.

PROPERTIES

Big hand (PUPIL)
Paper and pen (ALL)
Cheque (MR BIG)
Ten £50 notes (MR BIG)
Lineograph (PUPIL 6)
Peashooter (PUPIL 8)
Flower (VICTIM)
Sack of letters (HOSTESS)
Letters (TEACHERS 5 and 6, PUPIL 9)
Weather chart (WEATHERMAN)
Food, thermos, make-up, shower head (SHARON)
Violin-case, hockey-bag (JOANNE)

SOUND EFFECTS

Fanfare
Explosion
Chimes

THE ASSEMBLY SHOW

The front of a school stage, curtained, underlit and empty. Enter
COMPERE 1.

COMPERE 1: School Assembly. I hear you groan at these two
words. I said 'I hear you groan at these two words'.
(Loud groans from off-stage) Thank you. Think of it. Every day,
year after year, millions of innocent school-children are forced
to endure this dreary ritual.

Enter COMPERE 2.

COMPERE 2: Every day they have to wait for the same dull old
teachers to shamble on to the stage. Here they come now. *(A
few dull old* TEACHERS *appear and stand dully.)* Every day they
have to stare at the same dull old stage.
COMPERE 1: Every day they listen to a reading, drone a hymn,
mumble a prayer, hear a notice or two and shuffle out again.
COMPERE 2: Day after day, week after week, month after
month, year after year.
COMPERE 1: And then you wonder why today's youngsters are
growing old so quickly!
COMPERE 2: But do school assemblies have to be like this?
Couldn't they be more colourful, more exciting, more swingy,
more zingy?
COMPERE 1: We think they could. Shoo, you dreary, old-style
teachers! *(Exeunt* TEACHERS*)* And to prove that assemblies
can be different, we present to you now:
COMPERE 2: The amazing!

COMPERE 1: The amusing!
COMPERE 2: The astounding!
COMPERE 1: The resounding!
BOTH: The Assembly Show!

Fanfare. The curtains part to reveal a flashily colourful set suggesting a t.v. game. On one side are rows of seats with the pupils already seated. In the centre is Mr Big's desk (raised), and on the other side are the seats for the staff.

COMPERE 1: And now let's all get ready to give a great welcome to the star of the show!
COMPERE 2: It's the man himself, the guy you've all been waiting for: our headmaster: Mr Big!

Fanfare and wild applause. Enter HEAD.

HEAD: Well, thank you, thank you. My name is Mr Big and welcome to my Assembly Show; I know you're going to love it. Hi there, kids!
PUPILS *(loud)*: Hi there, Mr Big!
HEAD: I can't hear you!
PUPILS *(very loud)*: Hi there, Mr Big!!
HEAD: That's better. Today we have a super-duper programme for you: all our usual competitions with big-money prizes; music for everybody, jokes, sport, and a special guest-appearance from one of your favourite teachers, Miss Groovy! *(Cheers and whistles)* And we round the whole thing off with a surprise fashion spot. But first, I'd like you all to give a really warm-hearted welcome to the finest bunch of teachers in the universe: your friendly staff!

The STAFF dance in singing

STAFF: Here we come, your friendly staff,
Here we come today.
All we wanna do is make you laugh,
It's a great great time for play.
So all sit tight and don't be fright,

We're all gonna go, go, go.
You'll get your laughs from your super staff
In our great Assembly Show!

HEAD: All together now!

The PUPILS *join in the repeat of the song, changing pronouns.*
STAFF *sit opposite* PUPILS.

HEAD: Nice to see you all, you wonderful teachers. Now let's kick off with today's collection of Golden Oldie corny jokes.

TEACHER 1: I say, I say, I say, what lies on the bottom of the sea and trembles?

PUPIL 1: I don't know; what does lie on the bottom of the sea and tremble?

TEACHER 1: A nervous wreck!

ALL *groan*.

TEACHER 2: I say, I say, I say, what do you get if you cross a kangaroo with a sheep?

PUPIL 2: I don't know; what do you get if you cross a kangaroo with a sheep?

TEACHER 2: A woolly jumper!

ALL *groan*.

TEACHER 3: I say, I say, I say, why do Swiss cows wear bells round their necks?

PUPIL 3: I don't know; why do Swiss cows wear bells round their necks?

TEACHER 3: Because their horns don't work!

ALL *groan*.

TEACHER 4: I say, I say, I say, what is black, shiny, lives in bushes, and is very dangerous?

PUPIL 4: I don't know; what is black, shiny, lives in bushes and is very dangerous?

TEACHER 4: A blackberry with a shotgun!

ALL *groan*.

HEAD: How corny can you get? Give 'em a big hand!

A PUPIL *produces an enormous model hand, shows it to the audience, then presents it to the* STAFF. *More applause.*

HEAD: You've got to hand it to them! Time now for the sports results. Over now to our talented sports staff to bring us up to date. First, Mr Cruncher will fill us in on the rugby scene.

MR CRUNCHER *(wearing rugby kit)*: Your rugby teams all did well last week-end. The First XV played a new fixture against the Girls' High School. This resulted in a high-scoring game with plenty of excitement and some really committed tackling. Just one very slight complaint: the headmistress of the Girls' High School has written to ask if we would return their scrum-half. She was drawn into a loose scrum near the end of the game and did not re-appear. So if the First XV forwards could return the young lady, this game should soon become an established and attractive fixture.

HEAD: Thank you, Mr Cruncher. How did the girls' games go, Miss Harty?

MISS HARTY *(in track-suit)*: Jolly well. Now that we've switched to Rollerball, there's far more red-blooded excitement in the Saturday matches. Last Saturday, only two girls were killed *(groans of disappointment)* but all our teams won their matches. *(Applause)*

HEAD: Splendid, Miss Harty! As you all know, we have various swimming teams in school, and I'll ask Miss Fish to tell us all about it.

MISS FISH *(in flippers, etc.)*: I must say that the diving team did really well against St Vitus's Academy, in spite of several serious injuries. Next week we do hope to have water in the bath. Tomorrow after school we shall be staging another round of Mini-jaws. As most of the girls know, Mini-jaws is the new sport that's taking over from old-fashioned swimming galas. It's based on the film of *Jaws*, and it involves two teams of swimmers and a shoal of highly-trained piranha fish. These are trained to attack both human beings *and* first-form boys. I won't tell you any more; it might put you off your fish-fingers!

(Laughter and applause)

HEAD: Now, when we talk about games, we're usually thinking about outdoor games, but, you know, there are indoor games as well. *(One of the girls giggles.)* And I don't mean what you're thinking of, you saucy girl! So over to Mr Smoothly, who is waiting to tell us about indoor games.

MR SMOOTHLY: Hello, everybody. As we are rather short of playing-fields, we are experimenting this year with indoor games. Some of you are already practising corridor-racing between lessons; well done! This morning, we're going to try out roller-skating along the back corridor. Contestants will start from the Art Room and finish here on the stage. So over to our commentator.

COMMENTATOR *(with binoculars)*: Hello and welcome to our first roller-race along the back corridor. It's a fine day with no wind, and a good crowd has gathered to watch the start. The distance is 87 metres and the going is firm. I can see the first contestant coming up to the gate now. She's under starter's orders. She's off! (ALL *watch*.) No, it's a false start. (ALL *groan*.) She's being towed back. She's sweating slightly. She's quite still. The count-down.

ALL: Five! Four! Three! Two! One!

COMMENTATOR: She's off! She's going well! Here she comes!

A series of crashes are heard, and SKATER *appears with her head through the framework of a door.*

COMMENTATOR: Back to the drawing-board! Next week we'll try it with the fire-doors open!

HEAD: Absolutely fascinating. Now, everybody, we've had a complaint from some of our sports teams that they're not getting enough support. So let's all practise the school chant. Off we go!

ALL: One, three, two, four,
 Who are we for?
 School! School! School!
 Five, seven, six, eight,
 Who do we appreciate?
 School! School! School!
 We can't count, we can't spell.
 S! K! Double-O! L!
 School! School! School!

HEAD: Not bad. Now let's have it *loud*.

 (All repeat it very loud)

HEAD: Thank you, everybody, and thank you, sports staff.
 Now paper and pens out for your pools check. (ALL *produce
 paper and pen.*) The results of all last week's school matches,
 including snooker, arm-wrestling and moto-cross, were as
 follows: 10 home wins, 6 away wins, 5 score draws and 3
 no-score draws. Dividends are expected to be on the low side,
 so if you've 21 points or more on your coupon, get your claim
 in today at the school office. Meanwhile, let's hear it for last
 week's school's pools winner, and it's *again* J. Potwell, of Form
 2G, who correctly forecast the result of every single one of last
 week's school matches. (*Applause*. J. POTWELL *comes forward.*)
 Congratulations, J. Potwell. You even forecast correctly that
 one hockey-match would be abandoned after 32 minutes
 because of a broken water-main. Here's your cheque for £500.

J. POTWELL: Thank you again, Mr Big.

HEAD: Give him a big hand! *(Wild applause)* Tell me, J. Potwell,
 what is the secret of your astounding success?

J. POTWELL: I do it by cheating.

HEAD: What's that?

J. POTWELL: I cheat.

HEAD: Hear that, folks? He cheats! *(More applause)* In that case,
 J. Potwell, you have won not only £500 on our pools, but also
 this year's prize for the Biggest Cheat! Another £500 in crisp
 £50 notes! Give him another big hand!

(More applause. Everyone counts out the notes as MR BIG presents them.)

HEAD: Off you go, J. Potwell, to spend that well-deserved prize-money.

J. POTWELL *does a victory wave and exits.*

HEAD *(quietening everybody)*: A word in your ear, friends. I have just given J. Potwell some rather special trick money that explodes when it's put in the pocket. Wait for it!

There is a loud explosion and laughter as J. POTWELL is flung back on to the stage. He glares at MR BIG and resumes his seat.

HEAD: I loved it. Now for a complete change of mood, we'd like to present the 37th chapter of the Book of Ezekiel. Quiet, please.

READERS 1 *and* 2 *come forward.*

READER 1: 'The hand of the Lord was upon me and carried me out in the spirit of the Lord and set me down in the midst of the valley which was full of bones, and, behold, there were very many bones in the open valley, and, lo, they were very dry. And he said unto me:

READER 2: "Son of man, can these bones live?"

READER 1: And I answered: "O Lord, thou knowest." Again he said unto me:

READER 2: "Prophesy upon these bones, and say unto them: 'O ye dry bones, hear the word of the Lord.'" Thus saith the Lord God unto these bones: "Behold, I will cause breath to enter into you and ye shall live."

READER 1: So I prophesied as I was commanded, and as I prophesied, there was a noise and behold a shaking and the bones came together.'

ALL *sing 'Dry Bones' (briskly).*
(ALL sit, head down, hands on knees. Spread fingers on each 'dry'.)

15

1. Ezekiel connected them dry bones
2. Ezekiel connected them dry bones
3. Ezekiel connected them dry bones
4. I hear the word of the Lord

   (Tap right foot on ground)

5. Your toe-bone connected to your foot-bone,

   (roll feet out and back)

6. Your foot-bone connected to your ankle-bone,

   (kick right leg out)

7. Your ankle-bone connected to your leg-bone,

   (stand, still stooping)

8. Your leg-bone connected to your knee-bone,

   (slap right thigh)

9. Your knee-bone connected to your thigh-bone,

   (shake hips)

10. Your thigh-bone connected to your hip-bone,

    (straighten back)

11. Your hip-bone connected to your back-bone,

    (rock shoulders)

12. Your back-bone connected to your shoulder-bone,

    (roll head)

13. Your shoulder-bone connected to your neck-bone,

    (raise head)

14. Your neck-bone connected to your head-bone,

    (raise arms)

15. I hear the word of the Lord.

   (walk round)

16. Them bones, them bones, gonna walk around,
17. Them bones, them bones, gonna walk around,
18. Them bones, them bones, gonna walk around,

   (raise arms)

19. I hear the word of the Lord.

   (slowly lower arms)

20. Disconnect them bones, them dry bones,
21. Disconnect them bones, them dry bones,
22. Disconnect them bones, them dry bones,
23. I hear the word of the Lord.

   (Reverse of lines 5–15)

24. Your head-bone connected from your neck-bone,
25. Your neck-bone connected from your shoulder-bone,
26. Your shoulder-bone connected from your back-bone,
27. Your back-bone connected from your hip-bone,
28. Your hip-bone connected from your thigh-bone,
29. Your thigh-bone connected from your knee-bone,
30. Your knee-bone connected from your leg-bone,
31. Your leg-bone connected from your ankle-bone,
32. Your ankle-bone connected from your foot-bone,
33. Your foot-bone connected from your toe-bone,

   (spread fingers)

34. I hear the word of the Lord.

   (hands on knees)

35. I hear the word of the Lord.
HEAD *(reverently)*: That was wonderful, everybody. *(With sudden change of tone)*: Time for the commercial break now.

Chime.

PUPIL 5: Hey, kids, do you have problems writing lines for sadistic teachers? Do you find that your social life is ruined because you have to waste time writing lines out by hand? Hear how one scholar solved the problem:

PUPIL 6: I used to feel so miserable
       Sitting writing lines,
       But now I've got a 'Lineograph' *(produces it)*
       And now my life is fine!

PUPIL 5: Yes, if you suffer from line trouble, why not take a tip from this clever pupil and invest in a 'Lineograph' electronic line-writer? It writes 500 lines a minute in any hand-writing, it costs as little as £20, and you can buy it at Woolworths, W.H. Smiths, Crisps, Boots, Wellingtons, Sandals, Sling-back Casuals, Wedges, Vedges, Jam Roly-poly and After-Eight Mints, in snakeskin, imitation leather or cast-iron. Remember the name: Erm, erm, the name you can't forget, erm . . .

Chime.

PUPIL 7: Are you thin, spotty, fat, short-sighted, bandy-legged and knock-kneed? Does everybody avoid you because you're smelly and repulsive? Well, hard luck: it must be tough.

Chime.

HEAD: As headmaster of a large school, I often find it necessary to talk to my pupils about annoying habits, and there's one that seems very common at the moment. I'm talking about pea-shooters. Pea-shooters. This stupid habit not only wastes valuable food, it's not even dangerous. Let's see a demonstration of a normal, old-fashioned pea-shooter at work. *(To* VICTIM) Go off and walk back across the stage, would you? *(To* PUPIL 8) Now, you shoot him. (PUPIL 8 *produces pea-shooter and hides.* VICTIM *walks across the stage holding a flower and singing merrily.* PUPIL 8 *shoots, but there is no effect, and* VICTIM *walks off.)*

HEAD: You see? Absolutely harmless. Pick up those peas, would you? Now, let's watch the scene again, but this time we're *not* wasting peas.

(PUPIL 8 *holds up something different, which he loads into the pea-shooter.* VICTIM *reappears.* PUPIL 8 *shoots again. There is a loud scream from* VICTIM *who arches his back, falls and thrashes about screaming.*)

HEAD: Finish him off! (PUPIL 8 *kills him with another shot and the screaming stops.*)

HEAD: Jolly good. Take him away. *(He is carried off. Laughter and applause.)*

PUPIL 8: I was using a simple and cheap poisonous dart. It's easy to use, comes in five delicate pastel flavours, causes agonising death and is good for a real old laugh. It's obtainable at:

ALL *(singing)*: Your fabulous tuck-shop.

PUPIL 8: So buy a packet for your friends today at:

ALL *(singing)*: Your fabulous tuck-shop.

HEAD: Thank you, advertisers. Now back to our main programme, and it's over to the person who's transformed your R.S. lessons: the Reverend D.J. Brightly! *(Applause)*

REV. BRIGHTLY: Greetings, greetings. It's time for this morning's hymn, and we've had a whole sackful of requests since yesterday, so let's see who will be lucky today. Whose request will be first out of the bag? And let's hear it for today's hostess, who will choose the lucky letter.

HOSTESS *minces forward, smiles cutely, daintily picks out a letter, holds it up and presents it to* REV. BRIGHTLY, *who opens it.*

REV. BRIGHTLY: Ah! Are you there, Anthea Groomkirby of Form 5D? Because this request is for you, you lucky, lucky, girl. It's from Melvin Crossbottle, also of 5D, and he says it's to remind you of all the happy evenings that the two of you have spent on the river-bank together. How sweet! The hymn is 'Down By The Riverside', so let's all stand and crack the rafters with that fine old trans-Atlantic favourite, 'Down By The Riverside'.

ALL *stand and sing 'Down By The Riverside' with enthusiasm.*

ALL: I'm gonna lay down my burden,
    Down by the riverside
    Down by the riverside,
    Down by the riverside,
    I'm gonna lay down my burden
    Down by the riverside,
    I'll study war no more.
    I ain't gonna study war no more,
    I ain't gonna study war no more,
    I ain't gonna study war no more.

    I'm gonna burn all my school-books
    Down by the riverside
    Down by the riverside,
    Down by the riverside,
    I'm gonna burn all my school-books
    Down by the riverside,
    I ain't gonna study any more.
    Ain't gonna study, ain't gonna study,
    I ain't gonna study any more,
    Ain't gonna study, ain't gonna study,
    I ain't gonna study any more.

REV. BRIGHTLY: A wonderful hymn, and a wonderful rendition. Now back to our leader.

HEAD: Time now for Problem Page. Each week, our panel of experts read out letters from worried people and give them free and friendly advice. So let's hear our first problem.

TEACHER 5 *(standing)*: This is a short letter and it's signed 'Worried Full-back'. It says, 'Dear Problem Page, I enjoy playing rugby, but after the game the other players give me funny looks in the changing-room. They say I am the wrong shape for the game. What can I do?' Well, my advice to 'Worried Full-back' is that this problem is not going to go away as long as she insists on playing rugby. I think, Angela, that you should switch to hockey like the other girls.

TEACHER 6 *(standing)*: This second letter is also from a girl. She writes, 'Dear Problem Page, I am deeply in love with my Geography teacher. I cannot stop thinking about him, even in Geography lessons. I know that he likes me as well, because last week he kept me behind to talk to me. He said, "I've got to say this to you: I simply can't read your writing. Did nobody ever teach you to write properly, Sandra?" Surely this shows that he is interested in me? Signed, Louise.'

My reply is: 'Dear Louise, Your love is wasted on this man. He can't even remember your name, and is more interested in Geography than he is in you. Also he is three times your age. Why not try your History teacher instead?'

PUPIL 9 *(standing)*: We often get letters from people who dislike particular subjects. For example, listen to this one: 'Dear Problem Page, I hate Chemistry. I do not understand it properly and I loathe all the smells. Also I am frightened of the Bunsen flames and the acids. Do I have to keep doing it? Signed, Timid'. My reply is: 'Dear Timid, You will have to keep on with Chemistry. Firstly, you chose it; secondly, you may grow to like it, and thirdly, you are a Chemistry teacher, and are paid to do it.'

HEAD: Valuable advice there. Do keep on sending your letters to Problem Page. I always enjoy reading them, even the ones we can't read aloud. Now over to the Weatherman at the Weather Centre.

WEATHERMAN: Good morning to you. *(Displays chart.)* Yesterday's school weather was pretty much as we expected. Those colds winds persisted that I predicted along the back corridor, and are likely to do so as long as the outside doors are all left open.

Today's weather: starting mild with a few stormy outbreaks round Rooms 7 and 8. There will be deep depressions associated with tests in Physics and Chemistry, but by break these depressions should have moved into the Staff Room, resulting in high pressure and stormy outbreaks among the staff. At mid–day there will be a deep trough outside the dining-hall. This trough is for the use of fourth-form boys, as we are short of tables. There will be the usual showers in the changing-rooms. These may fall as sleet if the heating packs up again. As the week goes on, things should improve. Outlook: sunny with sunny intervals. Now back to Mr Big.

HEAD: Soon be time for your exams, kiddies. *(Groans from* PUPILS*)* Hey! Hold your horses! There's no need to moan at these fabulous new modern-style exams. To demonstrate just how much fun these zingy new tests can be we have with us the chick that all you guys voted for as 'The girl I'd most like to be kept in with': Tracy Frogthorpe. Give her a big hand! *(Applause)* And our guest teacher today is the little lady that all you kids voted as 'Teacher I'd most like to be kept in *by*'. Yes, it's the star of the English Department: Miss Groovy! *(Applause)*

GROOVY: Hi there, everybody!

PUPILS: Hi there, Miss Groovy!

GROOVY: Hi there, Tracy.

TRACY: Hi there, Miss Groovy.

GROOVY: Nervous, Tracy?

TRACY: Gee, no, Miss Groovy.

GROOVY: Hear that, kids? She's not nervous! Let's give her another big hand! *(Applause)* Now, you know the rules, Tracy, so let's go. The subject you have chosen is English Literature, and your first question is 'Who is your favourite author?' Your favourite author. Take it easy, Tracy, you've plenty of time: your favourite author.

TRACY: Er, Enid Blyton.

GROOVY: And Enid Blyton is correct! *(Wild applause)* Are you going to take the 50p, or are you going for the pound?

TRACY: I'll go for the pound.

GROOVY: She's going for the pound! *(Wild applause)* And your second question, for the pound, is: 'Which character in the books by your favourite author has big ears?' *(Pause)* Big ears. *Big ears?*

TRACY: Er, Noddy?

GROOVY: Noddy! Little girl, you're teasing teacher! Big ears.

TRACY: Big ears?

GROOVY: And she's right! 'Big Ears' is the answer we wanted! *(Applause)* And for £10 and your C.S.E. in English Literature – (TRACY *is waving and smiling at friends*) – Are you listening, Tracy? (TRACY *nods*) 'Who wrote The Collected Plays of William Shakespeare?' *(Pause)* Who wrote The Collected Plays of *William Shakespeare*?

TRACY: Er, Charles Dickens.

GROOVY: Very near, Tracy, but not quite right. *(Bell)* And there's the bell. You've won £5 in cash, a basket of groceries, and a holiday for six in sunny Barnsley! Give her a big hand, folks! *(Cheers)*

HEAD: Nothing to fear from these fun-style new exams, kids. And you'll want to be off to your lessons.

PUPILS: Oh, no, we won't!

HEAD: Oh, yes, you will!

PUPILS: Oh, no, we won't!

STAFF: Oh, yes, you will!

PUPILS *(singing to the tune of 'Here Comes The Bride')*: Oh, no, we won't.

STAFF *(also singing)*: Oh, yes, you will.

> They finish the song, and the KIDS end with a final shout of 'Oh, no, we won't!' Everyone laughs.

HEAD: I think your friendly teachers can take a hint there, kids, but in case any of you were thinking of drifting into a lesson later in the day, here's a selection of the sizzling stuff that your friendly teachers have on the menu for you.

TEACHER 1: In Art, we're hoping to start a pottery class, and in the Art Room there will be a demonstration of throwing pots.

TEACHER 2: And next door to the Art Room, a demonstration of catching them. *(Laughter)*

TEACHER 3: This week's study-theme is 'The rabbit', and also in the Art Room will be 'Drawing rabbits from life'.

TEACHER 4: In the Biology Lab., we shall deal with 'The reproduction of the rabbit'.

TEACHER 5: And in the Handicraft Room, 'How to make ten rabbit hutches in half-an-hour'.

TEACHER 6: In Cookery, 'Ten tasty rabbit dishes'.

TEACHER 1: And in Art, 'How to stop throwing pots and start making dishes to put rabbit pies in'.

TEACHER 7: In History, 'The history of the rabbit'.

TEACHER 8: In Chemistry, 'The chemistry of the rabbit'.

TEACHER 9: In Music, 'The music of the rabbit'.

HEAD: And in Assembly tomorrow, 'How to forget all you ever knew about rabbits and start enjoying yourself'. But enough of this nonsense. The senior mistress has something to say to you all. Mrs Elderberry.

MRS ELDERBERRY: Several of you have stopped me in the corridor recently and complained that our school uniform is getting old-fashioned. *(Shouts of agreement. The* HEAD *smiles.)* All right, all right. So Mr Big and myself got into a huddle about it *(whistles and shouts of 'oh!')*, and we decided to show you a few ideas before we make a final choice. So let's round off today's Assembly Show with a preview of what *you* might be wearing next year.

   Music.

With so many people in school these days, it's getting harder to remember names, but if we all followed Kim's example *(enter* KIM, *concealing name on T-shirt)*, there wouldn't be a problem. *(*KIM *turns and smiles. She's wearing a T-shirt labelled 'Hi! I'm Kim'. Exit* KIM. *Applause.)*

Getting to lessons on time is another worry for us all. As the school gets bigger, journey times get longer. People have been moaning to me that they just can't reach a class-room soon enough to grab their favourite seat on the back row or near to a window. Our next model has borrowed an idea from the corridor-racers. *(Enter* PAT *in roller-skating gear.* PAT *circles, waves and exits.)* And clever Pat can be first into dinners every time! *(Applause.)*

Our third model is Sharon, in a costume that she designed to solve two problems at once. *(Enter SHARON wearing large helmet and coat with vast pockets.)* Sharon's first problem was how to sit through those long, long, lessons without having to listen to the teacher. But thanks to her special helmet (SHARON *extends an aerial from her helmet)*, Sharon can listen to her favourite disc-jockey, or even chat to local lorry-drivers on the C.B. band. She tells me that her private call-sign is 'Sugar Baby'. And if she doesn't feel like listening, Sharon's pockets are big enough to hold whatever else she needs to while away those boring lessons. (SHARON *demonstrates as* MRS ELDERBERRY *talks.)* For example, she can carry food, a thermos-flask, make-up kit, shower-attachment and a host of all those other extras that no modern miss can do without. 'Bye, Sharon. *(Exit SHARON. Applause.)*

Janice reckons that uniforms should be striking and colourful, so here's how she thinks we should all dress next year. (JANICE *enters wearing very colourful and unusual clothes. Laughter and applause.)* Thank you, Janice. *(Exit JANICE.)*

And finally, we all know that fashions repeat themselves, so perhaps next year we shall all be wearing what our mothers or even our grandmothers, wore. If so, you may soon look like Joanne. *(Enter JOANNE, wearing full old-fashioned uniform. She wears glasses and carries violin-case, sports-bag, etc. Laughter and applause. Exit JOANNE.)*

HEAD: Well, thank you, Mrs Elderberry, for those fascinating glimpses into the future. And thank you all for being such a wonderful, wonderful, audience. It's time for mid-morning break now, and the tuck-shops, the bars and the betting-shops will soon be open, so let's finish our show as we always do. Grab hold of your partner and say bye-bye the happy way. That's all, folks, hope you've enjoyed it! A-one, a-two!

They all conga out, smiling and waving.

CURTAIN

FOUL PLAY AT SUNNY BAY

CHARACTERS

MR BING, *owner of Sunny Bay*
MRS BING, *his wife*
MARTIN, *a young postman*

BLUECOATS	*THE DOWN FAMILY*	
CARL	MR DOWN	
MARK	MRS DOWN	
ROB	BILLY	*twins*
TOM	BERNARD	
KATHERINE	KEITH	
HELEN	DIANA	
SUE	DAVID	*the smallest*
DOLORES		

GRANNIES	*VANDALS*
GERTIE	*VIC*
GLADYS	*SCOTT*
DORIS	*CHRIS*
BERTHA	*DARREN*
EMMIE	*INGRID*
FLO	*RUTH*

PROPERTIES

Hammers (MARK and CARL)
Cleaning things (KATHERINE and HELEN)
Shovels (ROB and TOM)
Clipboards (MR BING and DOLORES)
Three letters (MARTIN)
Whistle (MRS BING)
Luggage, including handbags (GRANNIES)
Luggage (DOWNS)
Sweets (DIANA)
Teddy (DAVID)
Teddy to contain bomb (CHRIS)
Knife/spray can (DARREN)
Pen (HELEN)
Signing-in book and pen (ON RECEPTION DESK)
Cheque (VIC)
Matchbox (CHRIS)
Lighter (SCOTT)
Menus (KATHERINE and HELEN)
Handbells (SUE and DOLORES)
Sign: 'CRAZY WALKS' (TOM and ROB)
Carrier-bag with bomb (VIC)
£5 and £1 (VIC)
Inflated balloons and pins (CHILDREN)
Drinks (GRANNIES)
Radio (FLO)
Letter (SUE)
Talent certificates (MR BING and HOSTESSES)

SOUND EFFECTS

Bells	Seagulls	Explosion
Epic music	Xylophone	Motorbike stopping
Bus stopping		

FOUL PLAY AT SUNNY BAY

*The sound of hammering. The curtain rises, revealing the reception area
of a holiday camp. It is the first day of the season. There are benches,
a reception-desk and a litter bin. Bunting has been strung up. CARL
and MARK are finishing putting up a sign which says 'Sunny Bay'.
KATHERINE and HELEN hurry on carrying cleaning things. Like
the rest of the staff, they wear overalls over their uniforms.*

HELEN: Oh, we shall never get it all ready in time.
KATHERINE: Come on, we've nearly finished.

*They hurry off. Enter ROB and TOM with shovels. They look
tired. CARL and MARK stand back to admire their sign.*

ROB: Where's the boss? Where's Mr Bing?
CARL: Worrying and scurrying as usual.
MARK *(pointing to the sign)*: He's going to like this.
TOM: He's not going to like what we have to tell him.
ROB: Come on, let's find him.

*They go out, passing SUE and DOLORES, who enter carrying
a signpost with several arms including 'leisure centre', 'swimming
pool', 'boating', 'kiddies' games', 'dancing' and 'beach'.*

DOLORES: Where does this go?
SUE: Here. *(They put it in place.)*

*MR BING hurries in. He wears a sombrero and carries a clipboard.
The girls giggle at his hat.*

DOLORES: Mr Bing. Is this right?

MR BING: Oh, very nice. *(To* MARK *and* CARL*)* That's very nice as well. Now, er, Sue, go and tell the other staff to meet me here. Immediately.

SUE: Will do. (SUE *and* DOLORES *go out.*)

> MR BING *looks round. A bell rings, a voice shouts 'Hello! Anybody there?'* MR BING *hurries off and returns with* MARTIN, *a young postman, who is holding a letter and looking puzzled.*

MR BING: It's late in the day for the post, isn't it?

MARTIN: Special delivery. *(He looks at the sign and shakes his head.)*

MR BING *(holding out his hand)*: What's your problem?

MARTIN: Well, this letter is addressed to 'The Owner, Sunny Bay Holiday Camp'.

MR BING: Right. My name is Mr Bing, I am the owner and this is Sunny Bay, sonny boy. (MRS BING *enters.*) And this is my wife, Mrs Bing.

MARTIN: But last year it was called Windy Bay, not Sunny Bay.

MRS BING: That's right. We changed the name. People like to go somewhere sunny for their holidays, don't they?

MARTIN: But it's not sunny, and it looks like rain. And why are you wearing that hat?

MR BING: Ah! It's Spanish, this. Helps to give the Continental effect. I'm practising a few Spanish phrases as well. Buenos Dias!

MARTIN: That's good. Say some more.

MRS BING: He's better things to do than speak Spanish to you. Have you no more letters to deliver?

MARTIN: Good thinking! I'll be seeing you! *(He starts to go.)*

MR BING: Oy!

MARTIN: Yes?

MR BING: My letter!

MARTIN: Your what?

MR BING *(holding out his hand)*: My letter.

MARTIN: Oops! Silly old me! *(He hands it over)* Byee! *(He goes.)*

MRS BING *(shaking her head)*: Where do they get them from?

Enter the rest of the STAFF, *chattering. They are still in overalls, etc.* MR BING *opens the letter and reads it.*

MRS BING: Quiet, please, everybody. Thank you. First, Mr Bing and myself would like to thank you all for working so hard to get the camp ready on time. But now we must all turn into hosts and hostesses and welcome our first guests of the season. The first ones should be here in half an hour. *(They all talk.* MRS BING *claps for quiet.)* So we've all just time to strip off our overalls –

MR BING: Oh, no! *(Reading)*

MRS BING: What do you mean, 'Oh, no'? We can't welcome them dressed like this.

MR BING: No. This letter. It's from the Lord Mayor. He's giving a prize for the best Holiday Camp in the area.

MRS BING *(taking the letter)*: Five thousand pounds, to be shared with the staff. *(Excited chatter)*

DOLORES: We're forced to win! We're miles better than the Super Cooper Camp, and that's the only other one with a chance, isn't it?

MR BING: Yes, but I don't trust Charlie Cooper. Remember last year? (MRS BING *nods grimly.)* He hi-jacked a coach-load of pensioners who were coming here. He's capable of anything.

HELEN: I think Super Cooper is a better camp than ours. *(The others disagree.)* Look at that swimming-pool they built last year.

MR BING: Right enough. He made those pensioners dig it. He pretended it was a keep-fit class, and most of them went home on stretchers. Still, it is a good pool.

MRS BING: There's no need to worry, love. Our pool will soon be ready, won't it? (MR BING, ROB *and* TOM *shake their heads.)* Why not? What's wrong?

MR BING: Damming and blasting is what's wrong?

MRS BING: Stop swearing! You're worse than Charlie Cooper!

ROB: He's not swearing, Mrs Bing. We'd nearly finished digging the pool next to the Leisure Centre when it happened.

MRS BING: When what happened?

TOM: We ran into rock.

MRS BING: That sounds very painful. Well?

TOM: Well, we need to use explosives to make a dam with the blast.

MRS BING: Now *you're* at it! Stop it!

TOM: We have stopped it, because we can't finish it without blasting.

ROB: And if we blast, we'll blow up the Leisure Centre. We should have dug it over there. *(He points in the opposite direction from the Centre.)*

    MARTIN *hurries in.*

MRS BING: So we have no pool? *(They shake their heads.)*

MARTIN: Another letter, Mr Bing. It says 'Urgent', so I really urged myself.

MR BING *(opening it and glancing at it)*: Oh, no!

    He bursts into tears. Everyone looks embarrassed. MRS BING *comforts him.*

MR BING: Now we've no chance. And we need the money.

    He gives her the letter. HELEN *snuffles loudly, then begins to weep, followed by the other girls.*

MRS BING *(to* HELEN*)*: What are you crying about? You don't even know what's in this letter.

HELEN: I can't help it: I just like a good cry! *(The other girls nod in agreement.)*

    MRS BING *produces a whistle and blows it. They all stop weeping and look up.*

MRS BING: That's the end of crying for today. Let's hear what this letter says. Here, you. *(To* SUE*)* Read it to us. *(*SUE *takes the letter and reads it aloud.)*

SUE: 'Just to remind you that every camp will be judged soon after it opens. Make sure that all attractions are ready for inspection.'

KATHERINE: That's not fair!

MR BING: Fair or not, if people want to use the pool, it should be ready for them.

KATHERINE: And how many guests are coming this evening?

MRS BING: Not many. Just one family and, er, a Joan Club.

KATHERINE: And what is a Joan Club?

MRS BING: I'm not too sure. Darby and Joan Clubs are for old men and women, so I suppose a Joan Club is just for old women.

MARK: Well, a lot of old women aren't going to go swimming; they're just going to sit and chatter and knit. Hey, that's poetry!

SUE: But what about this family? Their kids'll be wanting to swim as soon as they get here.

The others agree.

MR BING: Never mind. All we can do is be helpful and cheerful. Right? (*They agree.*)

MR BING: Big smiles! (*They smile.*) Good! Splendid! Keep smiling! Off you go to change!

The BLUECOATS *hurry off to change, chattering as they go. The* BINGS *look downcast.*

MR BING: How can we win this prize? Having no swimming-pool is bound to count against us.

MRS BING: And it's mentioned in the brochures and the plans. It's on that signpost. We'll have to pray for a miracle.

TANNOY: Attention all staff. Attention all staff. A minibus-load of guests is approaching at nought feet. Scramble, scramble, scramble.

Epic music. The STAFF *hurry back wearing their bluecoat uniforms. They line up. The music fades. The sound of a bus stopping.*

MR BING: Who is it, Dolores?

DOLORES: It's the old ladies.

The GIRLS say 'Aw!' sympathetically.

MR BING: You girls get ready to help these poor old ladies. I'll try a bit of Spanish on them for that Continental touch.

The BLUECOATS line up and smile. Enter GERTIE. Like all the GRANNIES, she wears a hat and coat and glamour specs and carries a handbag and suitcase.

MR BING *(kneeling)*: Bienvenido al Campo del Sol, senora.
GERTIE *(after lifting her hat-brim and staring at him)*: What's the matter with him?
CARL: It's Spanish.
GERTIE: More like rubbish. And what's it supposed to mean?
CARL *(kneeling)*: 'Welcome to Sunny Bay Camp, your ladyship.'
GERTIE: Well, why couldn't he say so? *(calling)* Hey, girls! This way!

The other GRANNIES enter, smiling and waving.

GRANNIES: Hello. Hello, everybody!
GERTIE: Hey, listen to this! *(To CARL)* Say it again.

The other boys grin at CARL, who looks embarrassed and kneels.

CARL: Welcome to Sunny Bay Camp, your ladyship.

The GRANNIES applaud.

GRANNIES: Very good! Isn't he sweet! He's lovely! etc.
EMMIE: Well, don't we get a welcome as well?
MR BING: Of course you do! *(He waves the others forward.)*
BOYS *(kneeling)*: Welcome to Sunny Bay Camp, your ladyships!

They stand. The GRANNIES embrace them with squeals of delight.

FLO *(kissing one)*: What a way to start a holiday!

The GIRLS smile at the boys' embarrassment.

DORIS: I feel younger by the minute!

BERTHA: And what's your name, pet?

ROB: Er, Robert.

BERTHA: Robert! That's my favourite name! Robert! Eeh!

FLO: Be quiet a minute, Bertha. Unless I'm mistaken, these lovely people are looking a bit puzzled. Now, what's wrong?

The STAFF *look at each other and smile in embarrassment.*

MR BING: To tell the truth, ladies –

GLADYS: If you tell the truth, young man, you won't get far in this life.

DORIS: You won't have much fun, either! (*The* GRANNIES *giggle.*)

GLADYS: Never mind them. Say what you have to say.

MR BING: Well, we all expected you to be quiet old ladies.

The STAFF *agree and the* GRANNIES *screech with laughter.*

EMMIE: Us, quiet! That's a laugh, isn't it, girls?

FLO: I'll say. Our neighbours are always kicking up a fuss because we're too noisy.

EMMIE: They're always saying 'Can't we have a little bit of hush'. Are you ready for a song?

MR BING: What, now?

GLADYS: Why not? There's always time for a song. This is one we made up on the bus, and it's called 'Can't We Have A Little Bit Of Hush?' Ready, girls? A-one, a-two!

GRANNIES: In olden times, as we've been told,
The young were young and the old were old.
The young had fun while the old sat by,
Did a bit of knitting and raised their cry:
'Can't we have a little bit of hush?'

Now, my friends, as you can see,
Things ain't like they used to be,
'Cause we have fun while the young sit by.
They listen to their trannies and raise the cry:
'Can't we have a little bit of hush?'

We can make the fellers squeal,
'Cause modern grannies got sex-appeal.
We spray our hair and we powder our noses –
We look like peaches and we smell like roses
And we never want a little bit of hush.

When the sun goes down and the lights switch on,
That's the time that we're turned on –
We love to dance and we love to sing,
In fact, we're game for anything –
Except for a little bit of hush. Hush!!

Applause.

MRS BING: Thank you, ladies. Now our hostesses will show you to your rooms.

GERTIE: Aw, can't the young men show us?

MRS BING: I'm afraid that it's the girls' job. Lead the way, Katherine.

The GRANNIES *moan, but go off cheerfully with the girls. The others laugh.*

MARK: Quiet old women! Ha!

MR BING: Anyone else coming, Mark?

MARK *(looking off)*: No, the road's empty.

MR BING: Good. Come on, boys, we'll put up some more lights on the pier. We can win that prize yet.

They go off. The stage is empty.

MRS DOWN *(off)*: Hello!

MR DOWN *(off)*: Hello!

ALL THE DOWNS *(off)*: Hello!

All the DOWNS, *except* DAVID, *appear, carrying their luggage. They are poor and look tired.* DIANA *is eating. They sit.*

MRS DOWN *(glaring at* MR DOWN *)*: Last time I'll take your advice!

MR DOWN: What?

MRS DOWN: 'We don't need to take the bus. It's an easy walk from the station.'

BERNARD ⎱
BILLY ⎰ : It wasn't easy, was it, mam?

KEITH: I feel sick, mam.

DIANA: I don't; I feel hungry.

BERNARD ⎱
BILLY ⎰ : You're a pig, you. You're always eating.

> DIANA *starts to cry. The others jeer.*

MR DOWN *(very loud)*: Shut it! Just shut it! Listen, all of you. Why have we come here? *(Silence)* Why have we come here?

KIDS *(muffled)*: To have fun.

MR DOWN *(loud)*: Why?

KIDS *(louder, but still weeping)*: To have fun!

MR DOWN: Right, and don't you forget it!

MRS DOWN *(panicking)*: Where's David? Where's my baby?

DIANA: He dropped his teddy and had to go back for it, little stupid.

MR DOWN: If he's smoking again, he'll catch it!

MRS DOWN *(rising)*: David! Oh, he's coming! Come on, lovey! Here we are.

> *Enter* DAVID, *sucking his thumb and carrying a large teddy bear. He is aged seven, but dressed to look younger.*

MRS DOWN: Come and sit on Mummy's knee, my angel! Here we are at the Holiday Camp. Aren't you glad?

DAVID *(shaking his head)*: I want to go home.

MR DOWN: It's going to be a real cheerful holiday, this, isn't it? *(To DAVID)* Here, you. Remember how old you are when they ask you. How old do you say? (DAVID *glowers at him.*) Are you seven?

BERNARD ⎱
BILLY ⎰ : Yes, he is.

MRS DOWN: Be quiet, you two. You'll spoil everything.

MR DOWN: Are you six? (DAVID *shakes his head.*) Five? *(Another*

shake) Four? Four? *(DAVID sullenly nods his head. The other
CHILDREN laugh mockingly and say 'Four!' MRS DOWN shushes
them while DAVID hides behind the seat.)*

Enter SUE and DOLORES, who carries a clipboard.

DOLORES
SUE }: Good evening! It's a happy day at Sunny Bay!

MR DOWN: You could have fooled me!

DOLORES: You must be the Brown family.

DOWNS: Down.

DOLORES: Brown.

MR DOWN *(standing)*: Down! *(Startled, DOLORES sits.)*

MR DOWN: No, stand up! *(She does.)* Our name isn't Brown,
it's Down.

DOWNS: Down! *(She sits, then smiles and rises again.)*

MR DOWN: Have you got it down?

SUE: We've got it down, but it's down as Brown.

MRS DOWN: Well, it should be down as Down, not Brown.

DOLORES *(altering the list)*: Down.

DOWNS: Down. *(Smiling and nodding)*

SUE: I think we'd better check the whole list again. Mr William
Br- Down. *(MR DOWN nods.)* Mrs Down. *(MRS DOWN
nods.)* I haven't got your first name, Mrs, er, Down.

MRS DOWN: Ida.

SUE: Mrs Ida Down. *(SUE and DOLORES start to laugh, but choke
it off as MRS DOWN glares.)*

SUE: Billy, aged twelve, and Bernard, aged twelve. Are you
twins?

BERNARD: I am.

BILLY: I am, as well.

SUE: Keith, aged eleven.

KEITH *(raising his hand)*: Fried things make me sick.

DOLORES: You don't have to have fried things, Keith. We'll
boil you an egg.

KEITH: Boiled eggs give me stomach ache.

MR DOWN *(shutting him up)*: All right!

SUE: And you must be Diana, aged ten? Are you looking
   forward to staying here, Diana? *(DIANA nods.)*
MRS DOWN: She doesn't say much.
KEITH: Too busy stuffing her face.
SUE: And David, aged four. *(She looks round.)* David, aged four.
MRS DOWN: That's right.
DOLORES: Where is the little chap? Has he come?
MR DOWN: David! Come here! *(DAVID emerges.)*
MRS DOWN: The young lady wants to know how old you are,
   David. Tell her. *(DAVID is silent.)* You're four, aren't you?
   Aren't you? *(DAVID nods. Relief all round)*
MR DOWN: There you are. Four years old.
MRS DOWN: That's two adults, four kiddies at half-price and
   one child under five sharing his parents' bedroom: free.
DOLORES: He's very big for his age, isn't he?
MRS DOWN: He is not. He's just young for his size.
DOLORES: Oh. Well, we'll show you to your rooms now.
   You're on Lloret Drive. Come along, David, and see your
   pretty cot. I hope it's big enough.

   They go out, DOLORES *still chattering.* DAVID *has left his
   teddy. The bell rings.* DAVID *returns and finds his teddy.*

TANNOY: Testing, testing, testing.

   DAVID *freezes and looks round.*

TANNOY: Can you hear me? *(DAVID nods.)*
TANNOY: Testing volume. Up, down. Up, down.

   DAVID *begins to exercise as the voice continues.*

TANNOY: Up and down and in and out,
             That's what camping's all about.
MR DOWN *(off)*: David! David! Come here!

   DAVID *runs off with his teddy. The bell rings again, longer this
   time. Enter* RUTH *and* INGRID, *who stand chewing and looking
   round.* INGRID *finds a pen and pockets it. They whistle and beckon.*

Enter the other VANDALS: VIC, CHRIS, SCOTT *and* DARREN. VIC *kicks a seat, then begins to jump on it. Enter* HELEN *and* KATHERINE. *The* VANDALS *stare sullenly at them, then slowly gather menacingly.*

HELEN: Can we help you?

VIC: No, I can smash it myself, thanks. *(The others laugh.)*

KATHERINE: It's a happy day at Sunny Bay.

INGRID: Oh, yeah? So what?

HELEN: Are you all staying here?

RUTH: Think you can stop us?

KATHERINE: No, everyone's welcome. Perhaps you'd like to sign in?

SCOTT: Perhaps we don't like signing.

HELEN: We just need your names in writing.

DARREN *(producing a knife/spray can)*: This is how I sign my name: watch! *(The others encourage him as he prepares to 'sign'.)*

KATHERINE ⎫
HELEN ⎭ : Stop it! We had to paint that!

MR BING *(off)*: Anything the matter?

DARREN *puts away the knife/can. Enter* MR BING.

MR BING: Buenas tardes! Good evening! It's a happy day at Sunny Bay!

SCOTT: What's he on about?

MR BING: Any problems?

VIC: Not yet, but give us a chance.

RUTH: Yeah, we're working on 'em.

MR BING: Er, good. I hope we shan't have any.

CHRIS: You keep hoping, Mister.

MR BING: You young people haven't booked, have you?

CHRIS: What's wrong with that?

MR BING: Nothing. Nothing at all. Here's the signing-in book, and there should be a pen – *(He looks on the desk while* INGRID *grins.* HELEN *gives him one.)* Ah, thank you. Sign here, please. *(The* GANG *sign.)* How long shall we have the pleasure of your company?

RUTH: Pleasure! *(The* GANG *laugh.)* Nobody's ever called it that before.

INGRID: One night, one place. Another night, another place. Get it, Mister?

MR BING *(looking at the book)*: Yes. I wonder if I dare ask you to pay in advance, then you can leave tomorrow without any fuss.

VIC: That's what we thought. Here's a cheque. All made out. Six of us. I think it's right?

MR BING: Oh, many thanks. *(Surprised)* This is exactly right.

HELEN: We'll show you your rooms.

SCOTT: Forget it. Where are they?

HELEN: Over there. Torremolinos Avenue.

CHRIS: You've got to be joking. See you tonight behind the Disco, darling. *(They start to go.)*

MR BING: Shall we bring your luggage?

CHRIS *(patting his pockets)*: No luggage. I travel light. *(He holds up a box of matches and shakes it.)* Light. Get it?

SCOTT: Hey, Mister, I travel lighter. *(He holds up a lighter.)* Lighter. Get it? Good joke, eh? *(They go out laughing.* MR BING *looks after them and shakes his head.)*

KATHERINE *(looking at the book)*: Look at these names!

MR BING: Names? What's wrong with them?

KATHERINE: V. Handel.

MR BING: What's wrong with that?

HELEN: It makes Vandal.

KATHERINE: And the rest are the same. S.M. Asher.

MR BING: That's Smasher.

KATHERINE: Chris Hallas.

HELEN: Callous.

KATHERINE: Darren Facer.

MR BING: Defacer.

KATHERINE: Ingrid Steel.

HELEN: I steal. She had the pen from the desk.

KATHERINE: Ruth Less.

MR BING: Ruthless. And look who signed their cheque!

HELEN: Charlie Cooper! He's sent them here to wreck our camp!
KATHERINE: Yes. So we won't win that prize.

The light is beginning to fade.

MR BING: I'll go and warn the staff to keep an eye on them.
HELEN: It's nearly bedtime. Perhaps they won't vandalise anything tonight.
KATHERINE: Good night, Mr Bing. Try and forget them.
MR BING: I'll try. 'Night, girls. Sweet dreams.

They go out. The lights fade, then come up again. Seagull noises. A bell rings. CARL and MARK hurry on.

CARL ⎱
MARK ⎰ : Wakey, wakey, rise and shine!
  The sun is up and the weather's fine.
  Let's all get up and start the day
  In a happy, hearty, healthy way.

Happy music. The GUESTS, led by TOM and ROB in track-suits, jog in, some in nightwear/dressing-gowns. They circle the stage and face front, looking tired.

TOM ⎱
ROB ⎰ : Raise your arms for half a mile,
  Shake them out and give a smile.
  Down and up and in and out:
  That's what camping's all about.

They jog on the spot. Enter the GIRLS dressed as cooks. SUE and DOLORES ring bells, the others carry menus.

MARK ⎱
CARL ⎰ : Hello, girls, what's the news?
KATHERINE ⎱ *(holding up menus)*:
HELEN ⎰ Bacon, eggs and grapefruit juice,
  Cornflakes, toast, coffee or tea.
  Come on, campers, run and see.
SUE ⎱
DOLORES ⎰ : Time for all of you to eat;
  Jog off now for a tasty treat.

GUESTS *and* STAFF *all jog off. Noise of eating in unison ('chomp, chomp, slurp, slurp'). A bell rings. They jog back on.*

KEITH: My eggs and bacon tasted greasy
ALL: Eggs and bacon tasted greasy.
CARL ⎫
MARK ⎭ : Never mind, just take it easy.
    Find yourself a space or chair.
    And breathe in deep that healthy air.

The GUESTS *sit on invisible chairs and breathe deeply in unison. Xylophone music.*

GIRLS *(singing)*: Breathe deep, go to sleep,
    Snooze in the breeze and sun;
    Cast your worries and cares away,
    And feel at ease at Sunny Bay.

Xylophone again. Seagulls. Ten seconds' peace. A very loud bell. They all leap up. TOM *and* ROB *run in and set up a sign: 'crazy walks'.*

TOM ⎫
ROB ⎭ : Hear that bell? Hear that chime?
    It's crazy competition time!

The GUESTS *turn away.*

    Now come on, folks, and don't be lazy;
    Show us a walk that's really crazy!

Five GUESTS *cross the stage doing comic walks.*

ROB: Number One: now ain't that fun?
TOM: Number Two: that can't be true!
ROB: Number Three: what do I see?
TOM: Number Four: bet your feet are sore!
ROB: Number Five: I said walk, not jive!
MR BING: That's your lot; there ain't no more.
    Let's hear applause for Number Four!

Applause. He makes a presentation to Number Four.

MRS BING: We hope that you enjoy your stay
      And all have fun at Sunny Bay.

TOM
ROB   } : Here's our brand–new Leisure Hall,
      So come on in and have a ball.

The GUESTS *and* BLUECOATS *begin to leave.*

HELEN
KATHERINE   } : Here are kiddies' games and rides;
      Roundabouts and swings and slides.

CARL
MARK   } : And moored down here for you to choose
      Are yachts and rowboats and canoes.

SUE
DOLORES   } : And each attraction that you see,
      Remember: it's completely free!

The stage is empty except for THE BINGS.

MR BING: I don't know how you keep your cool,
      We haven't got a swimming-pool,
      And how can anyone keep calm
      When those young toughs are up to harm?
MRS BING: You just have faith, my doubting pet,
      We'll win that competition yet!

They go out. Enter VIC *with a carrier bag. He looks round furtively.*

SCOTT *(off)*: Psssst! *(He enters.)*
VIC *(starting nervously)*: What do you do that for?
SCOTT: Do what?
VIC: Hissing like that. *(He imitates it.)* Sounds like a bomb just
  before it goes off.
SCOTT: Well, I'm not a bomb, am I?
VIC: No, but I've got one in here. *(He shows the bag.)*
SCOTT: Hey, it might go off! *(He starts to hide.)*

VIC: Come here! I haven't set it yet.

SCOTT: Well, set it then, and leave it where Charlie told us: in that Leisure Centre.

CARL and MARK stroll on. They inspect the area, including the litter bin, nod to VIC and SCOTT and go out.

VIC: See that? They're on to us. If I leave this bag, they'll find it before we've time to get away.

Enter INGRID, RUTH, DARREN and CHRIS furtively. They say 'Psssst!'

SCOTT
VIC } *(starting)*: Don't do that!

INGRID: Where's the bomb?

VIC: In here. *(They recoil.)*

DARREN: When is it going to go off?

VIC: It's not set yet.

DARREN: Charlie said set it for twelve o'clock, and it's quarter-to now.

CHRIS: Yeah. Set it and leave it. It makes me nervous.

SUE and DOLORES stroll in, looking around. The GANG look innocent. SUE and DOLORES go out. The GANG breathe again.

SCOTT: We can't just leave it; them bluecoats'll find it and defuse it.

RUTH: So what do we do? If we let Charlie down, he'll kill us.

SCOTT: I'm not scared of Charlie Cooper.

INGRID: No, you're too thick. There must be a way of hiding it so they won't find it.

They look round, then sit defeated.

CHRIS *(suddenly, standing behind VIC)*: Give us five quid!

VIC: Get lost!

CHRIS *(putting an arm round VIC'S throat)*: Give!

VIC frantically fumbles in his pockets and gives him the money.

CHRIS: Ta! *(Holding up the note.)* This'll do the trick! Set the bomb; I'll be right back. *(He hurries out.)*

DARREN *starts to take out the bomb. Enter the* DOWN CHILDREN.

KEITH *(loud)*: Hello!

DARREN *starts and hurriedly puts the bomb back.*

BILLY: What are you hiding in that bag?
RUTH: It's a surprise.
BERNARD: I bet it wouldn't surprise me.
VIC *(reaching for his wallet)*: How much do you want to bet?
RUTH *(to BERNARD)*: Take no notice of him.
DIANA: I bet it's got sweets in it, hasn't it?
RUTH *(nodding)*: Yes, you've guessed.
DIANA: Give me some sweets, 'cause our Mam and Dad won't buy us anything. *(To the others)* Will they?
KIDS: No, they won't.
DIANA: Let me see 'em, 'cause I guessed.

She tries to look. VIC *pushes her roughly away.*

DIANA: You hit me! I'm going to tell our Dad, and he'll tell them bluecoats, and they'll get you. *(She cries.* VIC *sighs and produces a pound. She stops instantly.)*
VIC: Here's a quid to buy some sweets. You won't tell the bluecoats, will you?

She shakes her head and takes the money.

BILLY: I want some money for sweets.
BERNARD: So do I.
KEITH: I don't, because sweets make me sick.
DARREN: And having you kids round here makes us sick!

Their faces start to crumple.

RUTH: Wait! Wait! Listen! All of you go down to the, er *(looking at the signpost)*, swimming-pool for a bit, then at twelve o'clock come to the Leisure Centre, and there'll be a surprise for all of you. It's what's in here.

TWINS: Promise?

GANG: Promise! Bye!

The CHILDREN *start to go out, and the* GANG *relax.*

DIANA: Come on, our David.

DAVID: I've left my teddy.

The teddy is under the seat, but no one has heard DAVID, *and* DIANA *pulls him out saying 'Come on!'*

CHRIS *reappears with another bear.*

CHRIS: New member of the gang!

VIC: You spent my five quid on that?

CHRIS: Yup. Set the bomb for twelve o'clock; we're going to hide it in this bear, see?

CHRIS *rips open the (velcro'd) back of the bear, pulls out a mass of cotton-wool and gives it to* SCOTT.

INGRID: Watch out!

Enter CARL *and* MARK. CHRIS *pares his nails,* DARREN *uses the bear as a puppet and says 'It's a grotty day at Sunny Bay',* VIC *replaces the bomb in the bag and looks away from it,* RUTH *and* INGRID *chew and stare upwards.* SCOTT *stares at the* BLUECOATS, *then at the cotton-wool.*

SCOTT *(with a sickly smile)*: I love candy-floss! Can't get enough of it. *(They nod and stare at him.)*

MARK: Don't let us stop you!

CARL: No, you enjoy yourself.

SCOTT *gives another sickly smile and takes a mouthful.*

MARK *(looking off)*: Those kids are going to the swimming-pool!

CARL: Head 'em off!

They run off. SCOTT *coughs out the cotton-wool and puts it all in the litter-bin. The others laugh, then stare at the bag.*

CHRIS *(taking the bomb out of the bag and giving it to* VIC): Set it, quick!

VIC *carefully sets the bomb while the others watch tensely.*

VIC: It's set. Twelve o'clock: Boom!
CHRIS: Put it in the bear! *(They do so.)* This'll wreck their stupid Leisure Centre. Let's go. *(They stand.)*
RUTH: They're coming back!

They sit. VIC *puts the bear behind him.* MARK, CARL *and the* DOWN *children return holding inflated balloons.*

CARL: All together!
KIDS: It's a happy day at Sunny Bay!
CARL: And what have we bought?
KIDS: Balloons!

The TWINS *prick their balloons behind the* GANG *who start nervously. The* OTHERS *let theirs fly about. They laugh at the* GANG'S *nervousness.*

BILLY: That scared 'em, didn't it?
BERNARD: Yeah, they're chicken.
MARK *(to* SCOTT): Hey, you!
SCOTT *(nervous)*: What?
MARK: Eaten all your candy-floss?
SCOTT: Aw, yes. *(He smiles and licks his lips.* KEITH *finds the cotton-wool in the bin and holds it up.)*
CARL: And what are we going to buy now?
KIDS: Sweets!
KEITH *(dropping the cotton-wool)*: I bet I'll be sick, Mister.
MARK: Course you won't. Who'll be first to the sweet-shop?

As the other kids run off with CARL *and* MARK, *shouting 'Me!',* DAVID *sees the bear behind* VIC. *He says 'Teddy!' and, unnoticed by the* GANG, *takes the bear as he runs off. The* GANG *relax for a moment.*

VIC *(feeling behind him)*: Somebody's nicked it!

RUTH: What?
VIC: That bear! It's gone!
DARREN: It can't have!

They panic. SCOTT *looks under the seat and finds* DAVID'S *bear.*

SCOTT: It's here! You'd dropped it, stupid. *(He gives it to* VIC. *Relief all round.)*
INGRID: How long before it goes off?
DARREN: It's ten to twelve now. Only ten minutes to go.
SCOTT: Well, dump it in the Leisure Centre and let's get out before it blows up.
CHRIS *(starting to take it, then turning)*: Suppose a kid finds it and takes it outside?

They nod and think.

INGRID: I know! Take it to the Lost Property in the Centre. Nobody's lost it, so nobody can claim it. Be quick!
CHRIS: Right, see you back here. *(He hurries off.)*
VIC: You girls, check our rooms. We'll wait here.

The GIRLS *run off.* VIC *looks nervously at his watch.*

Enter GERTIE, DORIS *and* GLADYS *carrying drinks.*

GERTIE: Eeh! Three young men, all on their own!

The GRANNIES *sit next to the* VANDALS.

GERTIE *(to* VIC): It's a bit quiet, isn't it? *(He nods.)* What we all need is noise and excitement, isn't it?

The BOYS *look at each other and start to rise.*

VIC: We have to go.
GRANNIES: No you don't! Sit down!
GERTIE: Have a drink! *(She gives him hers.)* Gladys, more drinks. *(*GLADYS *goes out.)* When you're young, life should go with a bang, shouldn't it?

Enter CHRIS, *who waves to the others.*

GERTIE: Hi there! *(Enter GLADYS with tray of drinks.)* Here's another lovely young man, Gladys! Give him a drink. *(They all settle with drinks. The BOYS look panic-stricken.)*

GLADYS: You're all quiet, aren't you?

THE OTHER GRANNIES *(off)*: Yoo-hoo!

They enter, also with drinks. FLO has a radio.

DORIS: We've some lonely young men here, looking for a bit of life! *(The other GRANNIES surround them with 'Eeh's and 'Aw's and offer them more drinks.)*

FLO: Let's have some music! *(The others agree. FLO switches on her radio.)*

RADIO VOICE: And here is a time-check. It's five minutes before twelve: eleven fifty-five. And now back to Record Roundabout. *(Music. Enter RUTH and INGRID, who beckon to the boys. RUTH taps her watch.)*

BERTHA: Look at these two! They need cheering up as well, don't they? Come on!

Squawking, the GRANNIES seize them and give them drinks. The VANDALS look round desperately for a means of escape, but the GRANNIES hang on to them.

EMMIE: Didn't I see you buying a teddy bear just now?

CHRIS: Me? Oh, er, yes, that's right.

EMMIE: 'Mary had a little lamb'

BERTHA: 'She also had a bear.'

FLO: 'I've often seen her little lamb'

GRANNIES: 'But I've never seen her bare!'

They screech with laughter.

FLO: Where is it?

CHRIS *(nervous)*: Where's what?

FLO: The bear!

CHRIS: Oh, the bear! I er, I bought it for Ingrid 'cause it's her birthday. *(He indicates INGRID. They look at her and smile.)*

FLO: It's her birthday! *(Reaction from* GRANNIES) Well, I vote we take them all into the Centre and treat them to another drink!

INGRID *(desperate, looking at her watch)*: No! I er, I think the bar closed at twelve!

FLO: Well, it's only two minutes to; time to buy the drinks. Off we go! (FLO *starts* 'Happy 'Birthday To You'. *The others join in and start to drag the* GANG *towards the centre.)*

DARREN: Not the Centre! There's a bomb in there!

MR *and* MRS BING *enter as the* GRANNIES *laughingly drag the* GANG *off.*

MRS BING: They all seem very happy.
MR BING: He said something about a bomb.
MRS BING: Just a joke.

SUE *runs in holding a letter, followed by the* BLUECOAT *boys.*

SUE: Mr Bing! Look at this letter! One of that gang dropped it!

MRS BING *snatches it and reads it. Enter* DAVID *with teddy.*

MRS BING: It's from Charlie Cooper. It says 'Dear Vandals, Plant the bomb on the tenth' – that's today! – 'Explode it at twelve o'clock.' What time is it?

MR BING: One minute to twelve. *(They look round hopelessly.)*

DAVID *(to MR BING)*: Hey, listen to my teddy. You're making a funny noise, aren't you, teddy?

MR BING *(not listening)*: That's right, lovey. *(To the others)* We must find it!

DAVID: Listen to it, Mister. (MR BING *absent-mindedly takes it.)*

MR. BING: It could be anywhere. It could be – Aaaaah!

(He freezes and stares at the teddy. HELEN *runs in.)*

HELEN: Mr Bing! They say there's a bomb hidden in a b– Aaaaah!

They all stare in horror at the bear.

RADIO VOICE: And the time now is just coming up to twelve o'clock.

MR BING *looks at the teddy, yells 'Get down!' and hurls it away from the centre. Everyone drops and screams. There is a loud bang and a hissing noise. They stand chattering and dusting themselves down. Enter the* GRANNIES *and the* DOWNS. *The* DOWN *children are laughing happily.*

Enter KATHERINE *and* DOLORES *from the direction of the explosion. They are both smiling dazedly.*

KATHERINE } : Mr Bing! *(He rushes to them.)*
DOLORES

MR BING: Girls! Are you hurt?

KATHERINE: No, no one's been hurt. But that bomb made a great big hole in the ground.

MR BING *(thoughtfully)*: Did it?

DOLORES: And water's pouring into it!

MR BING: Is it? *(He thinks for a moment, then climbs up to address the crowd.)* Quiet please, everybody. *(People shush each other.)* When you arrived, we promised that you wouldn't have a dull moment, and I'm sure you'll agree that today hasn't been dull! *(Laughter and agreement)* I know that you must have one or two questions to ask –

DAVID *(raising his hand)*: Yes. Where's my teddy? *(Laughter)*

MR DOWN: And where's the swimming-pool?

MR BING: I'm glad you asked me that. That bang you just heard – I think we all heard it? *(Laughter and agreement)* That bang was to mark the opening of our brand-new pool! *(Applause)* At this moment it's filling up, ready for the first swimmers. Another question is –

DAVID: Where's my teddy?

MR BING: Where is David's teddy? Now if David trots across to the Lost Property Office, he will find his teddy waiting for him! *(Applause. Exit DAVID.)*

The sound of a motor-bike. MARTIN *runs in wearing a crash-helmet and waving a letter.*

MARTIN: Mr Bing! Mr Bing! Another letter from the Lord

Mayor! It's marked 'Very Very Urgent', so I hurtled here on my motorbike.

MR BING *(reading the letter to the crowd)*: 'Dear Mr Bing, We have just heard the opening of your new pool, and as Mr Charlie Cooper has been disqualified from the Best Camp Competition for cheating, I am happy to tell you that the prize of £5,000 has been awarded to Sunny Bay.'

Cheers and applause. Enter DAVID *with his teddy.*

MRS BING: And here's the bear who helped us win the prize! *(Applause)* So to round off the fun, let's all sing our very own Sunny Bay song. All ready? *(They prepare to sing.)*

DORIS: Hey, what about the Talent Contest?

MRS BING: Which Talent Contest?

FLO: It says in your brochure that there is a Talent Contest every Friday. And it's Friday today.

MR BING: That's true, but we have so few guests this week.

MR DOWN: We have no talent in our family. *(The* DOWNS *agree.)*

BERTHA: But we have rehearsed a song specially for this contest, haven't we, girls? *(The* GRANNIES *agree.)* It's another of our very own.

MRS BING: In that case, we must all hear it.

GERTIE: Look who's hiding over there! *(She points off-stage.)* Come here, all of you! *(Enter the* VANDALS *shamefaced.)* Now, we're going to sing you a song, if you promise to be good. Do you? *(The* VANDALS *nod.)* I'm very pleased about that. You should be cheering people up, not blowing them up. Right, girls. Take a deep breath. This song is called 'Up-To-Date Grannies'. A-one, a-two.

GRANNIES: Most of you have got teeth missing:
     Spoils the fun when you feel like kissing.
     One thing that I love to see
     Is perfect dentures smiling at me.
       Teeth are out of date –
       Got it, mate?

You can't call your ears terrific –
They are hardly scientific.
We have really got it made
With a super hearing-aid.
    Ears are out of date –
    Got it, mate?

What do youngsters see in eyes?
Every pair is a similar size.
To put a spell on the opposite sex,
Wear a pair of glamour specs!
    Eyes are out of date –
    Got it, mate?

Another thing that makes us stare –
Most of you have boring hair.
To make a scene that's really big,
Just pop on a different wig!
    Hair is out date –
    Got it, mate?

What a worry when your bones can break
Sinews snap and muscles ache.
Life for us is just fantastic –
Every joint is made of plastic!
    We are up to date –
    Got it, mate?

MR BING: Thank you, Grannies. My hostesses will present you
    with Talent Certificates. *(They do so. Applause)*
MRS BING: And now can we sing our Sunny Bay song?
GERTIE: Of course we can. All of us together. *(To* VANDALS*)*
    You line up with us. *(The* GRANNIES *link up with the*
    VANDALS *and everyone sings. Tune: 'Camptown Races')*
GIRLS: At Sunny Bay we sing this song,
ALL: Doodah! Doodah!
BOYS: At Sunny Bay you can't go wrong,
ALL: Oh, doodah day!

GRANNIES: There's always something new to do,
ALL: Doodah! Doodah!
DOWNS: You can sail or swim in the ocean blue,
ALL: Oh, doodah day!
BLUECOATS: There's not another spot has what our bay has
  got. It's a peach of a beach and an ace of a place –
ALL: Oh, doodah day!
GIRLS: You can play inside if the weather's cool,
ALL: Doodah! Doodah!
BOYS: Or excavate a swimming-pool!
ALL: Oh, doodah day!
MRS BING: Our camp has won the crown, all thanks to Teddy
  Down,
GRANNIES: He's really rare, a super bear,
ALL: Oh, doodah day!

CURTAIN

THE BEST IN THE BOOK

CHARACTERS

SHEPHERD 1 (ABE)
SHEPHERD 2 (BEN)
SHEPHERD 3 (DAN)
SHEPHERD 4 (ELI)
SHEPHERD 5 (MAX)
SHEPHERD 6 (SAM)
KING BALTHASAR
KING CASPAR
KING MELCHIOR
ALI, *their cheerful servant*
JOSEPH
INNKEEPER
ROMAN SOLDIER

ANGEL 1
ANGEL 2
ANGEL 3
ANGEL 4
ANGEL 5
ANGEL 6
QUEEN ALTHA
QUEEN LALIA
QUEEN THORA
MARY
INNKEEPER'S WIFE
THREE CAMELS

SCENE 1: A hilltop near Bethlehem
SCENE 2: On the road to Bethlehem
SCENE 3: Outside the King David Inn

NOTE ON STAGING

If you want to avoid a gap between Scenes 2 and 3 and do not have
a traverse curtain so that you can set up Scene 3 beforehand, Ali
and the Angels can circle the stage singing a repeat of Ali's song
while the stable, signs and table are set up behind them.

PROPERTIES

Book and pencil (SHEPHERD 3)
Bottle and cups (SHEPHERDS)
Three caskets (KINGS)
Luggage (ALI)
Puncture outfit
Talcum powder   } (ALI)
Cycle pump
Playing cards (KINGS)
Money (ALI and THORA)
Three packets (QUEENS; ALTHA's *the biggest*)
Census book and pen (*on table; Scene 3*)
Luggage (MARY and JOSEPH)
Sweeping-brush (INNKEEPER)
Dishcloth (INNKEEPER'S WIFE)
Bubble-blower (ALI)

SOUND EFFECTS

Sheep
Angel music
Puncture (bang and hiss)

THE BEST IN THE BOOK

SCENE 1: *A hilltop near Bethlehem. Night.* SHEPHERDS 1 and 2 *are playing 'I Spy',* SHEPHERD 3, *who wears glasses, is reading,* SHEPHERDS 4 and 5 *are just sitting,* SHEPHERD 6 *is sleeping.*

SHEPHERD 1: I spy something beginning with S.

A sheep baas off-stage.

SHEPHERD 2: Sheep.

SHEPHERD 1: Yeah.

SHEPHERD 2: I spy something beginning with G.

SHEPHERD 1: Grass.

SHEPHERD 2: Yeah.

SHEPHERD 1: I spy something beginning with B.

SHEPHERD 2: Er, boulders. (SHEPHERD 1 *shakes his head.*) Big sheep? Er . . . er . . . er . . .

SHEPHERD 1: You don't know, do you? (SHEPHERD 2 *shakes his head.*) Do you give in? (SHEPHERD 2 *nods.*) Bethlehem.

SHEPHERD 2: Bethlehem? You can't see Bethlehem from here.

SHEPHERD 1: What's that light down there then? *(pointing)* That's the King David Inn. That's in Bethlehem, isn't it? Another point to me. *(Looking up in the same direction)* I spy something beginning with S.

SHEPHERD 2 *(looking at SHEPHERD 1, but not looking up)*: A sheep, flying.

SHEPHERD 1: No. A star. *(Pointing)*

SHEPHERD 2: Oh, yeah. *(He looks up.)* It's bright, isn't it? What star is it?

SHEPHERD 1: I don't know. Ask Dan; he's the expert.

SHEPHERD 2: Ey, Dan, what's that star there?

SHEPHERD 3: Which?

SHEPHERD 2: That one. That bright one.

SHEPHERD 3: Let's look in the book. Here: 'The night sky in December'. Is it near the Great Bear?

SHEPHERD 4: Yes, it's just below it.

SHEPHERD 3: Can't be; there isn't a bright star there.

SHEPHERD 4: Well, look then.

SHEPHERD 3 *looks up at the star, then back at his book.*

SHEPHERD 3: That's amazing. That's new. There shouldn't be a bright star there. It's not in the book.

SHEPHERD 5: What book is it anyway?

SHEPHERD 3: This is *The Observer's Book of Stars, Magic and Royalty*. It's got them all in, and I tick them off when I see them, but I can't tick one that isn't in. It doesn't make sense.

SHEPHERD 5: I think we've started to see visions. We've been up on this spooky hilltop so long that we're going crazy.

SHEPHERD 2: Yes, there isn't a new star at all; we're just bored out of our minds.

SHEPHERD 4: Could be; it's very boring being a shepherd. *(He sings, and the others join in)*:

> Being a shepherd is boring, boring;
> It's boring watching sheep. (SHEPHERD 6 *snores*.)
> And some silly shepherd starts snoring, snoring,
> If you try to sleep.

SHEPHERD 4 *(speaking)*: Wake up, Sam. (SHEPHERD 6 *awakes*.)

ALL *(singing)*: In the night it's extra boring,

> Nothing much to do but think.
> You can't watch the eagles soaring
> So have a little drop to drink. *(A bottle is produced.)*
> You don't hear the lions roaring *(They start pouring it.)*
> If you got a bottle of booze.
> Good to see it pouring, pouring;

Good ale is good news. *(They grow more cheerful and dance round.)*
Being a shepherd is *not* very boring,
Watching sheep is fun.
Of all the jobs in the whole wide world
Shepherding is Number One! *(They collapse in a happy heap. A sheep baas offstage.)*
SHEPHERD 6 *(throwing a stone)*: Be quiet!

The sheep baas once and is quiet. They laugh. Suddenly more sheep start to baa as a light shines on the SHEPHERDS *and strange music is heard. As they stare out front at the light, an* ANGEL *enters and stands behind them.)*

ANGEL 1: Don't be afraid.

The SHEPHERDS *think that one of them has spoken.*

SHEPHERD 6: I'm not afraid, kid.
SHEPHERD 5: I'm not either. I'm not scared of anything.
SHEPHERD 4: I'd fight a lion.
SHEPHERD 3: I'd fight a lion and a bear.
SHEPHERD 2: I'd fight a lion and a bear and wolf.
SHEPHERD 1: I would. Anyway, there's nothing to be afraid of.
ANGEL 1: That's right, Abe, there's nothing to be afraid of.

ANGEL 1 *steps slowly between them. The* SHEPHERDS *gasp. Then she slowly turns to face them. At the same time, the other* ANGELS, *unseen by the* SHEPHERDS, *appear behind them and silently surround them on three sides. The* SHEPHERDS *all whimper and huddle together.*

SHEPHERD 4: If you go away, I swear I'll never touch another drop.
SHEPHERD 1: It's like that star.
SHEPHERD 2: Yes, we're seeing things.
SHEPHERD 6: I didn't mean to hit that sheep with a stone just then. I like sheep really.
OTHERS: Yeah. That's right. Me too. I love sheep, *etc.*

ANGEL 1 *(slowly raising her arms)*: Be not amazed.

SHEPHERD 4: I'm getting out of here. *(The others agree. Slowly they edge away from ANGEL 1, then they turn to run, only to be confronted by the other ANGELS. They shriek and fall down.)*

SHEPHERD 5 *(raising one hand to ANGEL 1)*: Please leave us alone. We're only poor shepherds.

ANGEL 1 takes SHEPHERD 5's hand and touches each finger in turn. As she does so, the other ANGELS speak:

ANGEL 2: Unto you is born this day in the city of David

ANGEL 3: A Saviour which is Christ the Lord.

ANGEL 4: And this shall be a sign unto you –

ANGEL 5: You shall find the babe in swaddling clothes

ANGEL 6: Lying in a manger.

The ANGELS sing the first verse of 'O Little Town Of Bethlehem' then slowly walk off, humming the tune. Silence. SHEPHERD 5's hand has not moved. He stares at it. The light fades.

SHEPHERD 4: I didn't see anything.

SHEPHERD 6: Me neither.

SHEPHERD 1: I didn't either. I didn't see a lot of folk in white clothes.

SHEPHERD 2: With gold faces.

SHEPHERD 3: Singing.

SHEPHERD 4: Singing; yeah. I mean, no.

SHEPHERD 1: Ey, look at Max. Max! What's the matter?

Slowly MAX points at each finger in turn, then at one of the SHEPHERDS. As he does so, the SHEPHERD repeats part of what the ANGELS said:

SHEPHERDS: Unto you is born this day in the city of David
A Saviour which is Christ the Lord.
And this shall be a sign unto you –
You shall find the babe in swaddling clothes
Lying in a manger.

SHEPHERD 3 *(ticking his book)*: Those were angels. We must go

down to Bethlehem. We might see something else really good.
SHEPHERD 2: No, we can't leave the sheep. We should stay here.
SHEPHERD 1: Let's risk it. We shall always be sorry if we miss it.
SHEPHERD 5: We shall be more sorry if we get the sack.
SHEPHERD 4: Let's ask Sam. Aw, he's asleep again! Sam! Sam! Wake up!

SAM *shakes himself and looks at the others, still dazed.*

SHEPHERD 4: What do you think we should do, Sam; stay here with the sheep or go down to Bethlehem to see this Saviour?
SHEPHERD 6: Er . . . I think we should stay with the sheep *and* go down to Bethlehem.
SHEPHERD 5: And just how do we do that?
SHEPHERD 6: Easy; we drive the sheep down with us. All right?
OTHERS *(smiling)*: All right!
SHEPHERD 1: Let's go! Bethlehem, here we come!
SHEPHERD 5: Go on, you sheep. Go, go, go!

The sheep baa and the SHEPHERDS *pick up their things and go off, shouting at the sheep. As the noise dies away, we hear another sound offstage: it is the* KINGS *singing.*

SCENE 2: *Enter the three* KINGS *on their camels, carrying caskets and singing.*

KINGS: Being a monarch is boring, boring,
      It's awkward wearing a crown.
      We've spent ages touring, touring;
      It really gets you down.

      We're not keen on wearing fur,
      Specially now we're old.
      Carrying great big gifts of myrrh,
      Frankincense and gold.

When we get to Bethlehem,
Don't know what we'll see.
Could be an ordinary baby
Or a king like me.

There is a bang and a hissing noise. Melchior's CAMEL *staggers.*

BALTHASAR: Whoa! Everybody off!

They dismount painfully. Melchior's CAMEL *slowly collapses, hissing. The others watch it.*

MELCHIOR: My camel's got a puncture.

CASPAR: That's the fifth puncture you've had. Why do you have to ride a Japanese camel?

MELCHIOR: It's a hatchback.

CASPAR: Looks more like a hunchback to me.

BALTHASAR: Stop quarrelling, you two. You'll have to use a spare camel, Melchior.

MELCHIOR: We don't have a spare; just leave me to die here in the wilderness. And give the little baby my present. *(He sits and cries.)*

CASPAR: Stop crying! You're not going to die; we are going to mend the puncture. *(Shouts)* Ali!

ALI *(off)*: Yes, sire?

CASPAR: Come and mend this puncture, there's a good chap.

ALI *(offstage)*: Right away, sire. *(He enters carrying luggage. He inspects the fallen camel.)* Oh dear. We need a jack. Have you any jacks?

KINGS *(producing a card each)*: Three jacks!

ALI *(producing three cards, triumphantly)*: Three queens!

KINGS *(suddenly standing together with arms round each other's shoulders)*: Three kings! Pay up! *(Hands out)*

ALI *(to audience)*: You can't win them all. *(He pays them.)*

MELCHIOR: Stop wasting time, Ali. Can you mend this puncture?

ALI: I think so, sire, there is a puncture outfit. *(Takes out repair kit.)* But I must beg your aid.

CASPAR: Oh, very well. What do we have to do?

ALI: I don't know, 'cause I can't read. What does it say?

CASPAR *(reading)*: 'Roughen area round puncture with sandpaper.'

ALI: Very easy!

He rubs the CAMEL, *who screams, tries to rise and stamps on* MELCHIOR's *foot.* MELCHIOR *screams and falls.* BALTHASAR *and* CASPAR *hold it down.*

BALTHASAR: Stop screaming, you cowardly animal, or we'll leave you here to die. And you too, Melchior.

The CAMEL *and* MELCHIOR *moan and lie down.* BALTHASAR *and* CASPAR *pick up the instructions.*

BALTHASAR: Apply a thin coat of glue.

CASPAR: And wait ten seconds before applying the patch.

They count loudly from ten to one, then shout 'Zero!' ALI *slaps on the patch and the* CAMEL *screams again. The other* CAMELS *join in. The* KINGS *all shout* 'Shut up!' *and the* CAMELS *suddenly go quiet.*

BALTHASAR: Any more noise from you three and we'll be eating camel-meat tonight.

CASPAR: Yes indeed: Chili-con-camel! *(The* CAMELS *whimper.)*

ALI: Please, sires, have we finished?

BALTHASAR: Just one more thing: dust round the puncture with talcum-powder.

MELCHIOR: Here you are: *(reads)* 'Mr Macho. The talc specially made for males. Females wear it at their peril.'

BALTHASAR: Is this camel a male, Ali?

ALI: Oh, yes, sire. I borrowed it from the Post Office.

CASPAR: What's that got to do with it?

ALI: I am told, sire, that it says 'Royal Mail' on the back here.

All groan, including the other two CAMELS. ALI *applies talc all over the* CAMEL. *It also moans.*

ALI: Don't worry, you'll soon be all white.
MELCHIOR: Stop making weedy jokes and inflate this animal, I'm freezing.
ALI: Give me the inflator then, please, O sire.

> MELCHIOR *hands* ALI *a bicycle pump. He places the connector in the* CAMEL's *ear and slowly inflates it, all puffing. Gradually it rises.*

BALTHASAR: Well done, Ali. Now let's push on to Bethlehem.

> *Offstage is heard a female voice shouting* 'Darling!' *Then two others join in calling the kings' names.*

MELCHIOR: Who's calling?
ALI: I think it is the voices of your queens, O sires.

> *The* KINGS *groan. The* QUEENS *run on.*

ALTHA: Balthy!
LALIA: Caspy!
THORA: Melchy!

> *They embrace.*

CASPAR: But what are you three doing here? We thought you were back at home looking after our palaces.
ALTHA: I couldn't bear to stay at home, darling. I had to make sure that Ali was feeding you properly.
LALIA: We just had to come and see the little baby king that all the fortune-tellers are talking about.
THORA: And this place Bethlehem was featured in last week's holiday programme. It looked very attractive.
BALTHASAR: But how on earth did you follow us? We've travelled over –
CASPAR: Moor and mountain.
MELCHIOR: Field and fountain.
KINGS *(pointing)*: Following yonder star. O-oh –
> *(singing)* Star of wonder, star of light,
>   Star with royal beauty bright.

QUEENS: Westward leading, still proceeding,
      Guide us to thy perfect light.

THORA: We know the song, you see.

MELCHIOR: Oh. Well, you can't see the baby if you haven't brought a present for it.

ALTHA: And what presents have you brought?

BALTHASAR: I've brought gold!

ALTHA: Gold! For a baby!

CASPAR: And I've brought frankincense!

    The QUEENS *laugh.*

MELCHIOR: And I've brought myrrh!

QUEENS: Myrrh! *(They laugh.)*

BALTHASAR: Very well, if you're all so clever, what have you brought?

LALIA: I think I know about babies. I've brought a packet of nappies. *(Produces them from offstage.)*

THORA: What a coincidence, my dear: *I've* brought a packet of nappies too. I think *I* know about babies as well. *(Produces them.)*

BALTHASAR *(to* ALTHA*)*: Don't tell me: you've brought a packet of nappies because you *think* you know about babies.

ALTHA: No. I *really* know about babies.

BALTHASAR: So what have you brought?

ALTHA: I've brought *ten* packets of nappies. *(Produces a very large parcel.)*

    All laugh, including the CAMELS.

LALIA: But why are you all standing around here? We thought that you'd all be in Bethlehem by now.

CASPAR: Oh, we've just been mending this camel. It's ready to ride now.

THORA: How thoughtful of you! Thank you very much! *(The* QUEENS *move towards the* CAMELS.*)*

MELCHIOR: I think that you ladies should go back home straightaway. It's very bleak country up ahead. We may have to sleep tonight in a dirty hovel.

CASPAR: Or up a tree.

BALTHASAR: Or in a hole in the ground. We've hardly any money left.

LALIA: How sad. Well, come on, girls. If we set off now, we should reach Bethlehem by nightfall.

ALTHA: Yes, I'm looking forward to a warm room at the inn.

MELCHIOR: But suppose the inn is fully booked?

THORA *(showing money)*: Don't worry, dear, we have oodles of money, and money talks.

QUEENS *(singing)*: We like to be a queen,
We like to wear a crown.
It's lovely wearing jewels
And the latest gown.

We like to be a queen,
We like it being rich.
We always get a room
Without the slightest hitch.

And if we're feeling lonely,
If we're feeling low,
We whistle up a camel *(whistle)*
And off we go.

They mount and ride off repeating the second verse. Silence. The KINGS *and* ALI *look at each other.*

ALI: It's getting very cold, sires. We must start walking.

BALTHASAR: Yes, we must. Here you are. *(Gives* ALI *his casket.)* I'll see you in Bethlehem. *(He starts off.)*

CASPAR: Hey, wait for me! Here you are. *(He gives* ALI *his casket and follows.)*

MELCHIOR: Hey, don't leave me! *(He also gives his casket to* ALI *and runs off, shouting)* Wait! Wait! Don't leave me!

ALI: Sires! Kings! Queens! Highnesses! I can't carry all these! What's the baby going to say when he wakes up on Christmas morning and there aren't any presents in his stockings? *(To himself)* I've a present for him as well, but I'll never reach Bethlehem tonight if I have to carry all these. It's all right for

Royalty; they don't think about poor folk like me. *(He sits.)* I wish that I could fly over the mountains and get to the baby before 'em. That'd be a good laugh.

The bright light shines on him and we hear the angel music.

ALI: Cor blimey! *(He is dazzled by the light.)*

The ANGELS *enter behind him. Four pick up the luggage left by the* KINGS *and* QUEENS, *then the other two pick up* ALI *and seat him on their shoulders.*

ALI: Hey! Who's the star now? *(They begin to move off,* ALI *singing)*:
    And if you're feeling lonely,
    If you're feeling low,
    Whistle up an angel
    And off you go!

SCENE 3: *At one side: a sign, 'Welcome to Bethlehem'; next to it is a table, with some papers, a pen and a sign, 'Census', and a chair. Centre: the stable. The other side: an inn-sign, the King David Inn. Enter* JOSEPH *with luggage. He sees the Bethlehem sign and stops.*

JOSEPH: Bethlehem at last! It's a miracle! *(He puts down the luggage, calling)* Mary! We're there!
MARY *(entering and putting down her luggage)*: Bethlehem! I thought we'd never get here, Joe. I'm so tired.
JOSEPH: Me too. Look, there's an inn. I wonder if they have a room free.

The INNKEEPER *enters and sweeps in front of the inn.*

MARY: That's the innkeeper. Go and ask him, Joe.
JOSEPH *(crossing to the* INNKEEPER, *who keeps his back to him)*: Excuse me, have you any room?
INNKEEPER *(turning)*: What?
JOSEPH: Have you any room at the inn?

INNKEEPER *(pausing to think)*: I'm not sure. I'll ask the wife.
  (Shouts) Martha! *(To* MARY *and* JOSEPH*)* Have you come far?
JOSEPH: We've hardly stopped walking today.

  Enter INNKEEPER'S WIFE *carrying a dish-cloth.*

WIFE: Yes?
JOSEPH: We wondered if you had a room free.
INNKEEPER: They've been walking all day.
WIFE *(staring at the pair)*: Hmm. How many of you?
JOSEPH: Just the two.
WIFE: That your daughter?
JOSEPH: Er, no. It's my wife.
WIFE: She's a lot younger than you.
JOSEPH: Yes, she is.
WIFE: Hmm. Just for the one night is it?
MARY ⎱
JOSEPH ⎰ : That's right.
WIFE: Hmm. Most of our guests pay extra for our three-course
  meal.
JOSEPH: I'm afraid we can't afford that. Some soup would be
  nice, though.
WIFE: Oh, I don't know. *(Making up her mind)* All right. You can
  have the front room; it's the last we have. My husband will
  show it to you if you come inside. I have to finish the washing-
  up.

  INNKEEPER *and* WIFE *exit.* MARY *and* JOSEPH *hold hands
  and smile.*

MARY ⎱
JOSEPH ⎰ : There *is* room at the inn!
JOSEPH: Let's go and look at our room.

  They walk to the doorway. Suddenly MARY *stops and exclaims:*

MARY: Joe!
JOSEPH: What's the matter?
MARY: We've forgotten the luggage!

  They walk back and pick up their luggage.

JOSEPH: Good girl. We don't want this stolen; it's all we have. Come on.

They walk back to the inn-door and enter. As they do so, a ROMAN SOLDIER *enters and sees them.*

SOLDIER: Hey! You two! Come here!

They re-enter without their luggage.

JOSEPH: Are you shouting at us?

SOLDIER: Yes. Where do you think you're going?

MARY: We've just booked the last room at the inn.

SOLDIER: Never mind about that. You don't live in Bethlehem, do you?

JOSEPH: No, we're just here for the census.

SOLDIER: Well, just trot across to my desk then. This is where we do the census. *(He sits.)*

JOSEPH *(crossing)*: Can I answer for both of us? This lady's very tired. She needs a rest.

SOLDIER: She can rest as soon as we've done this and not before. Come here, young lady. (MARY *crosses slowly.*)

SOLDIER: Names?

JOSEPH: Joseph.

MARY: Mary.

The SOLDIER *writes their answers down.*

SOLDIER: She your daughter?

JOSEPH: Wife.

SOLDIER: Wife, eh? Both family of David are you? *(They nod.)* Just the two of you?

JOSEPH: At the moment, yes.

SOLDIER: And what does that mean? Are there some others with you? *(He looks round.)*

JOSEPH: No, but, er, we have a baby on the way.

SOLDIER: Oh, I didn't realise. When's it due, Miss, er, Missis?

MARY: Well, any time now. Could we go to our room now, please?

SOLDIER: Just wait a minute. I have to put down everyone in the family of David who's here for the census. There's two of you now, but there might be three tomorrow. Or four if you have twins.

MARY: Oh, no there'll only be the one.

SOLDIER: You seem very sure.

MARY: Oh, yes, the angel told me.

SOLDIER *(staring at her)*: Come again?

MARY: The angel appeared and told me.

Unseen by JOSEPH and MARY, the three QUEENS appear, see the inn-sign and dismount. The INNKEEPER and his WIFE appear in the doorway. During the next speeches they mime a conversation. At first the WIFE is doubtful, but when they show her their bags of gold she smiles, takes the gold, and ushers them inside. Her HUSBAND leads the camels into the stable and tethers them. MARY'S and JOSEPH'S luggage is thrown out of the door.

SOLDIER *(to JOSEPH)*: You're right; she does need a rest.

MARY: The angel was all in white, with a gold face, like nothing I've seen before.

SOLDIER *(nervously)*: Yes, I'm sure. I think I'll just put the two of you down. *(Writes slowly.)* You'll be Numbers 1342 and 1343. Then if the baby arrives while you're here, let me know and I'll put him down on the list. Or her, of course, if it's a girl.

MARY: No, it's going to be a boy. And I know his name.

SOLDIER: Oh. I suppose the angel told you that as well?

MARY: That's right. How did you know?

We hear the angel music. Unseen by the SOLDIER, the ANGELS appear. Two are carrying ALI; the others carry the three caskets and one packet of nappies. They put down their burdens and stand smiling.

SOLDIER: And I suppose this 'ere angel had wings and all dressed in white with a gold face. *(Or describe the ANGELS on stage who smile and exit leaving ALI.)*

MARY: You must have seen an angel yourself.

SOLDIER: You must be joking. There's no such things as angels.
  (He finishes writing.) Well, that's that. You can go inside and
  have a rest. And good luck with the baby.
MARY: Thank you. We'll let you know if he's born here.
JOSEPH: Come along, Mary.
SOLDIER: Ey!
JOSEPH: Yes?
SOLDIER: These your camels?
JOSEPH: No, I haven't seen them before.

As they cross to the inn, the SOLDIER *is staring at the* CAMELS.

SOLDIER *(to himself)*: These aren't angels, are they?
ALI: No, they're camels.

The SOLDIER *sees* ALI, *then turns away looking puzzled. There
is a whistling noise and a packet of nappies comes sailing through the
air and hits him. He exclaims and turns to* ALI.

SOLDIER: Who threw that?
ALI: Not me.
SOLDIER: Well, it wasn't these two, was it? It's jail for you!
ALI: Honest, it wasn't me.
SOLDIER: Don't tell me it was an angel, all in white with a gold
  face, like nothing you've seen before.
ALI: Oh, no, it wasn't any different from the other five.
SOLDIER: What other five?
ALI: The other five angels. They were all standing there, just
  now.
SOLDIER: Well, knock me down!

*The packet of ten nappies comes whistling through the air and
knocks him down. He yells.*

SOLDIER: I'm getting out of here! Count me out! *(He runs off.
  The* CAMELS *laugh.* MARY *and* JOSEPH *smile and walk across to
  the inn. Then they see their luggage outside.)*
MARY: Joe, someone's put our luggage outside.
JOSEPH: Just the innkeeper cleaning up.

They pick up their luggage and prepare to enter. The INNKEEPER'S WIFE *appears. It is growing dark.*

WIFE: Yes?

JOSEPH: You said that you had a room free.

WIFE: We *did* have a room free, but you didn't take it, did you? I've given it to three proper ladies. They came here on those camels *and* they want a three-course meal as well. It's your own fault. Good night.

MARY: Wait! Where can we go?

WIFE: I don't know. All the other inns are full to bursting.

She shuts the door and goes in. MARY *starts to cry.*

JOSEPH: Mary, don't worry: we'll find another inn.

MARY: They're all full: she said so.

ALI: Hey, mister. Are you looking for somewhere to stay for the night? (JOSEPH *nods.*) Well, what about this stable?

JOSEPH: A stable? With those camels?

The CAMELS *turn and look at* JOSEPH *and* MARY.

ALI: You could do worse: it's dry, and you can keep warm in the straw. And it's clean straw. Isn't it, camels? *(The* CAMELS *nod.)*

JOSEPH: I suppose it's the only shelter in the town. Come on, Mary. *(To* ALI) Are you coming in as well? You'll be welcome. (ALI *hesitates, then nods and follows them into the stable. The lights dim except for the star over the stable.)*

It grows lighter. The ANGELS *enter singing the first verse of 'Away In A Manger'. They stand in front of the stable then part to reveal* MARY *sitting holding the* BABY *while* ALI, JOSEPH *and the* CAMELS *stand behind. Baas offstage. Enter* SHEPHERD 1.

SHEPHERD 1: Good morning, all!

OTHERS: Good morning.

SHEPHERD 1: We're seeking a baby that some angels told us about.

ALI: Angels! Were there six of them?

SHEPHERD 1: That's right!

ALI: They certainly get around, these angels.

SHEPHERD 1: Is this the right baby? My friends want to see it. They're over there *(pointing)* with our sheep. (SHEEP *baa.)*

ALI: Oh, dear. Yes, it's the right baby, but we've just got him to sleep and we don't want your animals to wake him up. You'd better stay away.

MARY: Why not put them in the field at the back? Then you can come and see the baby.

SHEPHERD 1: Good idea, lady! *(shouting)* Ben! *(The others shush him.)* Oops! Sorry! I'll be back. 'Bye! *(He runs off.)*

OTHERS: 'Bye! *(The* SHEEP *baa* "Bye'.*)*

    The QUEENS *enter from the inn.*

THORA: I shan't come here again! Those beds weren't fit for servants.

ALTHA: And I'm sure that cream wasn't fresh.

LALIA: Look, there's Ali!

ALI *(bowing)*: A very good morning to your Highnesses. Here is the baby that you are seeking. He is already attracting great interest. Very great.

THORA: We haven't travelled all this way to see a baby peasant; we can see those in the streets at home.

LALIA: We've come to see a special baby king.

ALTHA: Sweet and special, not lying with those dreadful camels. *(The* CAMELS *turn away.)* Where is the palace in Bethlehem?

ALI: The big houses are all up the hill, that way. *(He points past the inn.)* You can walk there in five minutes.

ALTHA: Walk, walk, walk? Why must we walk?

LALIA: Because it's less painful than riding on those camels, dearie. Off we go.

    They start to move off. The CAMELS *blow raspberries. They turn.*

THORA: Oh, Ali, if our husbands arrive, tell them where we are.

ALI: Yes indeed, your Highnesses.

They go out. The KINGS appear from the other side.

BALTHASAR: Bethlehem at last!

CASPAR: And there's Ali! And are those our camels? *(The* CAMELS *nod.)*

ALI: Greetings, your Highnesses. You have just missed seeing your wives.

MELCHIOR: Well, that's one minor miracle at least.

BALTHASAR: But, Ali, how on earth did you come here before us?

ALI: Oh, I didn't come on earth, sire; I found a secret way. Top secret. Very top. But here is the special baby that you are seeking, with his special mum and dad. Very special.

MELCHIOR: And we left our presents with you. How annoying.

ALI: Have no fear, sire; your presents are all present. And correct. *(He points.)* Very correct.

BALTHASAR: Well done, Ali. When we return home, you shall have a little gift.

ALI: Very little.

BALTHASAR: What did you say?

ALI: I said very little, your Highness. In fact, nothing at all.

CASPAR: If we are going to get home in time for the peasant-shooting, hadn't we better hand over our gifts and worship the baby?

MELCHIOR: Very true.

The ANGELS *sing the first verse of 'Once In Royal David's City' as the* KINGS *come forward to present their gifts. Meanwhile, the* SHEPHERDS *enter.*

SHEPHERD 5: Look at that!

SHEPHERD 2: Who are they, Dan?

SHEPHERD 3 *(taking out his book)*: Let me look in the book.

SHEPHERD 6: The six at the back have white robes and gold faces like those we saw on the hilltop.

SHEPHERD 3: Aw, shucks, they're just angels. Probably the

same ones. I've got them.

SHEPHERD 2: What about the three with crowns? They look like kings. I bet you haven't seen *them* before.

SHEPHERD 3: Wow! The one with the gold is called King Caspar, and the one with myrrh is King Balthasar, and the other must be King Melchior. They're all Eastern kings; I've never seen kings of that class in this area before.

SHEPHERD 1: And what about the others?

SHEPHERD 3: They're just peasants and servants. They're not listed in the book because they're not worth anything.

BALTHASAR: Excuse me, madam, have you chosen a name for him yet?

MARY: Yes. His name is Jesus.

SHEPHERD 3: Jesus! *(He crosses to them and kneels.)* Did you say that your baby is called Jesus?

JOSEPH: Yes, he is.

SHEPHERD 3: And you are his mother and father?

JOSEPH: That's right.

SHEPHERD 3: Hey!

JOSEPH: Why are you so excited?

SHEPHERD 3: Because Jesus is Number One! He's the best in the book! He's the only one in the Messiah class. That's amazing! *(He ticks them off in his book.)* Thank you for coming here! *(To the others, who have come nearer.)* This baby is the Messiah!

OTHER SHEPHERDS: The Messiah!

SHEPHERD 6 *(To* MARY): We know that we ought to give him presents, lady, but we've come straight from work.

ALI: My friends. *(They look at him.)* There are your presents. *(He points to the* QUEENS' *parcels. The* SHEPHERDS *exclaim. As they pick up the parcels,* ALI *takes a bubble-blower from his pocket.)*

ALI: I also have a small gift for the baby, madam.

MARY: Thank you, Ali. What is it?

ALI: Watch! *(He blows bubbles.)*

ALL: Aaaah!

ALI: A tiny piece of magic for your baby. And I think that the shepherds have some useful gifts for you.

The SHEPHERDS *present their gifts as the* ANGELS *clap, then they line up with* SHEPHERD 1 *at the end.*

CASPAR: Soon we must return to our own countries, but before we go we should sing a song to the newborn king. What shall it be? *(Pause)*

ALI: 'I'm Forever Blowing Bubbles'. *(The others shush him. Pause)*

SHEPHERD 1: I know! 'We Wish You a Nappy Christmas'! *(The others stare at him and shush him. Pause)*

CASPAR: I propose that we sing 'Silent Night'.

BALTHASAR: Very suitable.

The SOLDIER *enters, sees the* BABY *and says* 'Ah! Number 1344'. *As he writes in the book,* SHEPHERD 3 *says* 'He's Number One in my book'. *The others shush them and the* SOLDIER *lines up with them. The* WIVES *enter and say their husbands' names. The others shush them and they line up.*

BALTHASAR: Now, is everyone here?

ALL: Yes!

CAMELS: What about the innkeeper and his wife?

All turn, then laugh so loud that the INNKEEPER *and his* WIFE *come out. The others beckon them into the group.*

BALTHASAR: *Now* is everyone here?

CAMELS: Yes!

BALTHASAR: At last. We shall sing the first verse of 'Silent Night' in English. Ready?

They all, including the CAMELS, *sing the first verse of 'Silent Night'.*

CURTAIN

THE CLASS STRUGGLE

CHARACTERS

MRS ROSS *(a senior teacher)*
MR COREN *(a young teacher)*

BOYS	*GIRLS*
JACKSON	DEBRA
KAYE	ALISON
LISTER	GLENYS
MILSOM	SUSAN
PITCHLEY	JANET
BALDWIN	OLIVE
EGGSWORTH	SHARON
HUDSON	YVONNE
FLETCHER	KATHERINE
GOSNEY	ROSE
CARSWELL	ELIZABETH
ALEXANDER	JENNIFER

NOTES ON STAGING

The best place for the teacher's desk, cupboard and record-player is down-stage at one side. Use as few desks or tables as possible to suggest a class-room, otherwise movement will be difficult. If the pupils can sit in two rows with an aisle between the boys and the girls, the seating-order could be as in the list of characters, with the first six boys and the first six girls on the front row (stage right to left) then Eggsworth sits behind Jackson, Sharon behind Debra and so on. To help visibility, the back row can be on a shallow rostrum, or can be seated on higher stools. The entrance should be upstage, and the best place for the teachers to stand is in the aisle, where possible, rather than at the desk.

PROPS LIST

Books (ALL)
Coins (SHOVE-HALFPENNY PLAYERS)
Newspaper (GOSNEY, etc.)
Girls' paper (ROSE, etc.)
Musical paper (YVONNE)
Chewing-gum (GLENYS)
Sweets (BALDWIN)
Crisps (KAYE)
Pop (HUDSON)
Cigar (GOSNEY)
Collecting-tin (KATHERINE)
Keys (COREN)
Brief-case containing cigarettes, lunch-packet and unbacked note-book (COREN)
On the back wall: School rules
On or near teacher's desk: Books including dictionary and register, hand-bell.
Teacher's corner: Waste-bin, record-player, record.

THE CLASS STRUGGLE

A class-room. Most of the class are already in.

> *One group of boys,* JACKSON, KAYE, LISTER *and* MILSOM, *are playing shove-halfpenny on a front desk.* ROSE, KATHERINE, ELIZABETH *and* JENNIFER *are reading a girls' paper.* SHARON *is doing* YVONNE's *hair.* EGGSWORTH, FLETCHER, GOSNEY *and* HUDSON *are also reading a paper.* JACKSON *scores, evoking a cheer from the spectators. He does a victory salute and shouts 'I am the greatest!'*

SHARON: Aw, shut up, Jackson. And you sit still, Yvonne, or we'll never have you looking lovely.

> *There is a chorus of giggles from the girls reading the paper.* HUDSON *mimics them.*

KATHERINE: And you be quiet, Hudson. He'll be here soon.
HUDSON: Who cares?

> JACKSON *scores again and repeats his victory dance and shouts. Enter* MRS ROSS. *The class go quiet.*

MRS ROSS: Good afternoon, Jackson.
JACKSON *(sheepish)*: Afternoon, Mrs Ross.
MRS ROSS: Good afternoon, Fletcher.
FLETCHER: Good afternoon, Miss.
MRS ROSS: Could I have your attention, please? I've had two complaints from teachers recently about the behaviour of this class. Now, I was rather surprised because I enjoyed teaching you last year. Though some of you can be rather lively, can't you, Gosney?

GOSNEY: Yes, Miss.

MRS ROSS: So I don't want any more complaints. All right, Glenys? (GLENYS, *chewing, nods.*) Now, it's Friday afternoon and it'll soon be the week-end, so just see if you can keep your noses clean. Get ready for your lessons.

Exit MRS ROSS. *The shove-halfpenny players drift to their places.*

SUSAN: What's she on about? (GLENYS *shrugs.*)

Enter DEBRA, *looking depressed, and* ALISON.

ALISON: Ooh, Debra, I'm glad my mother's not like yours.

DEBRA: Honestly, Alison. She tells me to help her, and when I say 'I've got to do my homework' I don't think she knows what I'm talking about. I hope Mr Coren doesn't ask me to say that poetry we had to learn, 'cos I just don't know it.

SUSAN: I haven't learned any flipping poetry. What good is it?

GLENYS: Yeah, it's stupid.

SHARON: Don't worry, Debra. He'll have forgotten he set it. He usually does.

BALDWIN, *a small boy, rushes in, sits and looks round.*

BALDWIN: Cor, I thought I was late again. *(He sits grinning.)*

EGGSWORTH: Have you read this, Smiler? A bloke rode from Land's End to John o' Groat's in less than two days on a push-bike.

BALDWIN: Yeah, I saw it when I was taking my papers out this morning.

PITCHLEY: I thought you just took papers after school.

BALDWIN: Mornings as well now. I'm saving up for a proper racing-bike.

GLENYS *(sorting books)*: What lesson is it now?

SUSAN: English, Mr Coren. All afternoon.

GLENYS: Oh no, I'd forgotten. I hope he's in a good mood.

SUSAN: Some hope. He's always worse on a Friday afternoon.

OLIVE: I used to like English with that other teacher.

ELIZABETH: Coren's not bad. He's a bit strict, though.

SUSAN: I can't stand him. He's always yapping on about school rules.

ELIZABETH: It's the boys that make him worse, Gosney and that lot.

GLENYS: Well, he ought to shut them up, it's his job.

HUDSON *(pointing at the paper)*: Hey, look at this.

EGGSWORTH, FLETCHER, GOSNEY *and* HUDSON *burst out laughing at what they are reading.* HUDSON *thumps the desk. The others join in, in unison.*

SHARON: Shut up!

GOSNEY: Get lost!

GIRLS: Shut up!

BOYS: Get lost!

ALEXANDER *goes to the door. The two sides continue to shout, the noise building in a crescendo. Suddenly* ALEXANDER *waves his arms and yells out.*

ALEXANDER: He's here! Coren's here!

The noise subsides. COREN *enters. They stand. A long pause while he stares at them from the entrance.* HUDSON *snorts with laughter.*

COREN: What's the matter with you, Hudson? *(No reply)* Well?

HUDSON: Nothing.

COREN: Nothing, what?

HUDSON: Nothing, sir.

COREN *goes to his desk and puts his brief-case down.*

COREN: Sit down. I have to make a phone call. I'll be away for about five minutes.

GLENYS *is chewing.* COREN *picks up the waste-bin and pushes it at her.*

COREN: Spit it out.

> GLENYS *rolls her eyes, sighs, and wearily drops the gum in the bin.*

COREN: Look, Glenys, the school rules say that you don't chew gum.

GLENYS: Me?

COREN: Anybody.

GLENYS: It doesn't harm anybody.

COREN: Oh no? Yesterday some goon parked their gum on a radiator and it took me half-an-hour to get it off a girl's cardigan. *(Some of the boys snigger.)* It's not funny! I'm warning you lot! *(All look blank except BALDWIN, who is wearing his usual smile. COREN strides to him.)*

COREN: You! What are you grinning at, Baldwin? Stand up! *(BALDWIN stands.)* Well? What's so funny?

BALDWIN: Please, sir, I don't know, sir.

COREN: You don't know. It couldn't be because you're glad to miss part of my lesson, could it!

BALDWIN: Please, sir, I don't know, sir.

COREN: Could it?

BALDWIN: Sir, I've said: I don't know.

COREN *(shouting)*: Don't be insolent with me, lad! You'd better stay in tonight after school!

BALDWIN: Sir, I can't stay in. I've got a paper-round, and I'll be sacked if . . . .

COREN: Don't you tell me what you can't do! The school rules say that I can punish you by detention, or lines, or both. You'll stay in tonight and write out 500 lines! *(Gasp from class.)* And the rest of you, just watch out or you'll be punished as well, especially you two, Fletcher and Gosney! Now shut up while I'm away.

> *Exit* COREN. *Silence.* BALDWIN *starts sobbing.*
> ALEXANDER *keeps watch.*

PITCHLEY: Poor old Smiler. Will you really lose your paper-round? (BALDWIN *nods.*)

GOSNEY: He's mad, he really is, he's crackers.

FLETCHER: He's stark staring bonkers.

GOSNEY: And he's getting worse.

SHARON: You boys make him worse. If you go on making all that noise, he'll keep us all in.

HUDSON: I wonder what he did before he came here. I bet he was an animal-keeper at a zoo.

EGGSWORTH: Yeah, or a prison warder.

JACKSON: No, I'll tell you what. He was a concentration-camp commander. Did you see that film last night? *(Some nods)* Well, he looks like that German officer. *(Grins and nods.)* I bet that's what he was. Yeah! When they shot them prisoners with their machine-guns. *(He mimes it.)* It was great. They were blasting off with their guns and shouting.

KAYE: Achtung! Ze prisoners are revolting! Gun zem down!

JACKSON *and* KAYE *jump on their chairs and machine-gun the class. The boys and some girls fall screaming and moaning. A few girls look superior and don't react, including* SUSAN, GLENYS, JANET *and* OLIVE, *who say, 'Bang, bang, you're dead. Very funny, ha ha.'*

KAYE: Be upstanding! *(The ones who 'died' do so.)* It says in the rules that no-one can die without permission. Be down-sitting. *(They sit.)* Goot! all peoples will write out a million lines. *(Laughter)*

JACKSON *(striding across to* SUSAN *and the others)*: You! Why are you not obeying the rules like the other swine?

SUSAN: You're just not funny, kid.

JANET *(standing)*: You lot are always mocking Mr Coren behind his back, but it's you who make him get mad. If you think he's that bad, you ought to do something about it.

KATHERINE: Talk sense. What could they do about him?

JANET: Well, they could go to Mrs Ross about him. *(General groans)*

SHARON: Ma Ross'd just back him up. She'd have to.

GLENYS: Old Rossy's as bad as him, in any case. *(General disagreement)*

ALISON: Oo, she's not, she's nice.

JANET: I still think we should try and do something about him. He really frightens me sometimes when he loses his temper.

ALISON: It's not just him, though. I don't think half the teachers know we're human. Nobody treats human beings the way they treat us sometimes.

GLENYS: Nobody treats animals the way they treat us sometimes.

ELIZABETH: Yeah, they'd be prosecuted if they did.

HUDSON: Yeah! The R.S.P.C.A. could show pictures of us all badly treated and over-crowded. *(The boys huddle together gibbering 'Oh, we're over-crowded. Oh, we're badly treated. Help! Help! Spare a copper.')*

KATHERINE: Well, that's the first thing to do, isn't it?

ELIZABETH: What? Prosecute him?

KATHERINE: No, we ought to try and show him how miserable he can make us. I mean, look at Smiler.

PITCHLEY: Yeah, he's not smiling now.

ELIZABETH: It does make you wonder why Mr Coren gets so mad sometimes. Why should anyone act like he does?

JENNIFER: He might have indigestion.

MILSOM: I bet he never comes up on the pools.

LISTER: No, I bet his wife nags him a lot.

OLIVE: I don't think he's married.

LISTER: He is, I think.

MILSOM: He can't be.

HUDSON: Well, we've got to get him married, then. That's all we have to do. It'll give him an out–of–school interest. Keep him off the streets.

GOSNEY: Nobody'd marry him.

CARSWELL: Except a blind woman.

ALEXANDER: Or a deaf woman.

GOSNEY: Or a mad woman. *(He gibbers.)*

KATHERINE: Look, you're all just acting daft again. Can we do anything to stop Mr Coren going on the way he does?

SUSAN: No, we can't because he was born that way.

Pause. Some start reading again, etc. Suddenly KAYE stands.

KAYE: I know! I've got it! Listen! You know what Coren's always saying?

JACKSON: Yeah. 'The school rules say—'

KAYE: No, not that. He's always saying 'Repeat exactly what I say.'

BALDWIN: Yes. 'Repeat exactly what I say.'

ALL *(turning to neighbours)*: Repeat exactly what I say. Repeat exactly what I say.

JACKSON: All right, Coren says that; so what?

KAYE: Well, we'll do that. When he says it, we'll do it. He can't blame us for doing what he says.

GOSNEY: Say that again, kid.

KAYE: When he tells us to repeat what he says, then we repeat everything he says. Right?

GOSNEY: Yeah. All right. Let's practise, then. Baldy, you be Coren.

Different pupils imitate COREN with gestures, becoming noisier.

BALDWIN: Don't you be insolent with me!

ALL: Don't you be insolent with me!

GLENYS: Stop chewing! Spit it out!

ALL: Stop chewing! Spit it out!

MILSOM: What's this rubbish?

ALL: What's this rubbish?

ALISON: You're driving me crazy!

ALL: You're driving me crazy!

ALEXANDER: He's here!

All sit. Enter COREN.

COREN: The school rules say when a teacher is late, the class should work quietly. If you want to run around and scream, you should do it at home before you come to school. What should you do, Baldwin?

BALDWIN: Please, sir . . . .

COREN: Stand up when you speak to me. It's the only evidence
I have that you're not asleep. *(BALDWIN stands.)* What should
you do?

BALDWIN: Please, sir, run round and scream at home.

COREN: Really? Our friend Baldwin thinks that we should run
round and scream at home. When should we scream?

ALEXANDER: Please sir, never.

COREN: Good. *(He pats ALEXANDER's head and looks round.
ALEXANDER steals his keys.)* No intelligent person raises his
voice. We're not all football hooligans, are we, Carswell?

CARSWELL *(standing)*: Sir, no, sir.

COREN: You're a fool, Carswell. What are you?

CARSWELL: Sir, a fool.

COREN: Quite right. Sit down. Now, I seem to remember that
I asked you all to learn about sixteen lines of poetry, of your
own choice, for homework. Any volunteers? *(Silence)* Come
on, somebody must be anxious to entertain us. *(SHARON
raises her hand.)* Sharon.

SHARON: Sir, does 'Frankie and Johnny' count?

COREN: I don't see why not. Go ahead.

SHARON: 'Frankie and Johnny'.

Frankie and Johnny were lovers.
Oh my Gawd how they did love!
They swore to be true to each other,
As true as the stars above.
He was her man but he done her wrong.

Frankie went down to the hock-shop,
Went for a bucket of beer,
Said: 'O Mr Bartender,
Has my loving Johnny been here?
He is my man but he's doing me wrong.'

'I don't want to make you no trouble,
I don't want to tell you no lie,
But I saw Johnny an hour ago

With a girl named Nelly Bly.
He is your man but he's doing you wrong.'

That's fifteen lines, sir.

GOSNEY: Aw, let her finish it, sir, it's good.
COREN: Another day. I want to hear somebody else. *(He looks round the room; the class are all staring forward.* DEBRA *drops her eyes.)* Ah, Debra. A few lines of poetry from you. Stand up. *(Silence)* You have learned some, haven't you? *(*DEBRA *nods.)* Well, what's it called?
DEBRA: Er, 'The Daffodils.'
COREN: Oh, Wordsworth.
DEBRA: I think it's another man.
COREN: Go on, then.
DEBRA: Fair daffodils, we weep to see
　　　　You haste away so soon.
　　　　As yet the early-rising sun
　　　　Has not attained his noon.
　　　　Stay, stay,
　　　　Until the hasting day . . .
COREN: Go on.
DEBRA: The hasting day . . .
COREN: Yes?
DEBRA: Please, sir, I hadn't time to learn any more because I had to help my mother . . .
COREN: No excuses; you're another fool. Can't even remember a few simple lines of verse. What are you?
DEBRA: Sir, a fool.
COREN: A forgetful fool. What is she, Yvonne?
YVONNE: Sir, a forgetful fool.
COREN: Good. Everybody tell Debra what she is.
SOME BOYS *(enjoying themselves)*: Fool. Another fool. Forgetful fool, *etc.*
COREN *(banging on the desk)*: When I tell you to repeat what I say, I mean exactly what I say. I can see that you all need practice in elementary repetition. *(As he says this, he turns away*

from the class. KAYE *signals to them.)* Right, all of you, repeat exactly what I say.
ALL: Exactly what I say.
COREN: Don't be stupid!
ALL: Don't be stupid!
COREN: *Shut up!*
ALL: *Shut up!*
COREN: *Quiet!*
ALL: *Quiet!*
COREN *(banging his desk)*: *Stop it!*
ALL *(banging desks)*: *Stop it!*

Pause. COREN *looks round. They are all expressionless. He smiles stiffly.*

COREN: All right. Joke over.
ALL: All right. Joke over.

Another pause. FLETCHER, HUDSON *and* GOSNEY *stand.*

GOSNEY: We're fed up with you.
FLETCHER: Cheesed off.
HUDSON: Gorgonzola'd.
COREN *(gesturing)*: Sit down.
ALL *(mimicking him)*: Sit down.
COREN: Sit down, you three.
GOSNEY: Make us. *(Grins from the class)*
ALEXANDER: Ma Ross!

MRS ROSS *enters. The class stands.*

MRS ROSS: Good morning again, class.
ALL: Good morning, Mrs Ross.
MRS ROSS: You're all looking very happy at your work. Sit down. Oh, Mr Cohen, have you finished the article that you were writing for the School Magazine?
COREN: Oh, no, it slipped my mind. I'm sorry, Mrs Ross, I'll do it for Monday.

MRS ROSS: If you can. The printer's crying out for it. By the way, I thought I heard shouting coming from this room, anything wrong?

COREN: Yes, I . . . . No, just a little Drama.

MRS ROSS: Drama! Very good. You must all do a play for the rest of the school at the next concert. *(Crossing to* COREN.*)* Any problems?

COREN: No, thank you.

MRS ROSS: You're worried about your wife, I dare say? *(*COREN *nods.)* Well, jolly this lot along for an hour and then it's the week-end. *(At the door)* Well, class, I'll leave you to your little Drama. Good afternoon.

ALL: Good afternoon, Mrs Ross.

Exit MRS ROSS. *Pause.*

COREN *(quickly)*: All right, we'll have no more silly nonsense, and you should all be glad that I didn't report you to Mrs Ross. Now lets's get on with the lesson. Take out your writing books. I want you to write an essay on 'Respect for Authority'.

OLIVE: On what, sir?

COREN: Stand up when you ask a question!

ALL: Stand up when you ask a question!

COREN: Don't be insolent!

ALL: Don't be insolent!

COREN *(banging on the desk and speaking quickly)*: This is your final chance to behave. Do you want Mrs Ross to come back?

EGGSWORTH *(standing)*: Do you?

COREN: What?

EGGSWORTH: Do you want her back?

HUDSON *(standing)*: You don't want her to see that you can't control us, do you, sir?

COREN: On the contrary, I should be glad if Mrs Ross came back to see what a pack of hooligans you all are.

GOSNEY *(standing)*: Right, we'll get her back for you, mate. *(Starting to chant)* Come back, Mrs Ross. On your feet, everybody, join in. Come back, Mrs Ross!

Gradually, the rest of the class rise and join in until everyone is chanting loudly:

ALL: Come back, Mrs Ross. Come back, Mrs Ross.
COREN: Go on, you're making fools of yourselves!

The class continue chanting louder, stamping and drumming on the desks.

COREN: *Stop it!* Please.

The noise stops. MRS ROSS *enters. The class rise, smiling.*

MRS ROSS: Could you reduce the noise a little, Mr Coren? I know this class can get very enthusiastic, but it could disturb other classes. Carry on the good work. Thank you, Alexander.

Exit MRS ROSS. ALEXANDER *shows her out then locks the door, holding the keys up for the class to see, as* COREN *sits, head lowered.*

JENNIFER: You didn't tell her what a pack of hooligans we are, sir.
ELIZABETH: You wouldn't like us to get her back and tell her, would you, sir?
COREN: No, please. All right, work quietly on your own, it's obvious that I can't teach you anything.
ROSE *(standing)*: Well, if you can't teach us anything, sir, perhaps we can teach you something.
KATHERINE: Good idea. What lesson shall we teach him, then? *(Standing)* Any ideas?
COREN *(standing)*: I don't know what you're talking about.
KATHERINE *(to ROSE)*: He doesn't know what you're talking about.
CARSWELL: He's too stupid to learn.
GOSNEY: He'll just have to learn the hard way.
FLETCHER: The modern way.
HUDSON: The experimental way.
EGGSWORTH: The do-it-yourself way.

KAYE: The hell-on-earth way.

COREN: You're being absolutely ridiculous. I'm the teacher. What can you teach me?

DEBRA: We could teach you what it's like to be at school.

BALDWIN: And how we really suffer when you lose your cool.

OLIVE: And when the teacher tells you that you're nothing but a fool.

JENNIFER: Fool, fool, forgetful fool.

ALL: Fool, fool, forgetful fool. (*Three times in a crescendo ending in 'Hey!' and laughter.*)

HUDSON (*to the boys*): Here!

> *The boys huddle in consultation.*

FLETCHER: Right. Now? (HUDSON *nods.*)

> FLETCHER, GOSNEY *and* HUDSON *march out and tip the teacher's desk over.*

FLETCHER: There, sir. Stand inside that.

COREN: What?

FLETCHER: This is an interrogation, sir.

HUDSON: You are the prisoner, sir. Do you swear on the *Heinemann English Dictionary* to tell the truth, the whole truth and nothing but the truth?

COREN: Oh, all right. We'll have a mock trial if you like.

KAYE: Answer 'I do'.

COREN: I do.

JACKSON: You're going to enjoy this, sir.

> *The class begin to crowd round.*

GOSNEY: Get back and sit down. (*Most of the class sit on desks.*) If you've anything to say, then put your hand up. Right, carry on.

EGGSWORTH: Good evening. We are fortunate in having with us a distinguished teacher. His name is Mr Coren.

JANET: What's his first name?

EGGSWORTH: And the first question, Mr Coren, is what is your first name?

COREN *(after a pause)*: Er, Gerald.
SUSAN: Gerald!

There are some giggles and calls of 'Hello, Gerald'.

GOSNEY: Shut up! Carry on.
EGGSWORTH: Gerald has kindly consented to answer questions on any subject.
YVONNE: Are you married? *(COREN nods.)*
GLENYS: Why did you get married?
SUSAN: Yeah, your wife must be stupid.
GOSNEY: Shut it! Ask him proper things. *(Pause)*
LISTER: Can I ask him about school rules?
FLETCHER: Yes. What do you want to ask him?

LISTER *takes the rules from the wall.*

LISTER: You are always quoting these rules, Sir Gerald, so you must think that they are good?
COREN: Yes, I do.
LISTER: Every single rule?
MILSOM *(grabbing the list)*: Do you agree with every one of these 72 rules?
COREN: Well, perhaps not every single one.
MILSOM: Ah! Which rule do you disagree with, sir?
DEBRA: Yes, which?
COREN: Er . . . Well, I can't actually think of one, off-hand. *(General groans)*
MILSOM: First he says he doesn't agree, then he says he does. He must be a fool.
CARSWELL: Are you a fool, Mr Coren?
COREN: Look, this has gone far enough! If we're having serious questions, well and good, but insulting me isn't part of your education. We're going to resume normal lessons.

As he tries to lift the desk back, the class begin to chant 'Come back, Mrs Ross!' COREN suddenly runs to the door, to find it locked. He searches for his keys.

COREN: Where are my keys? Who's got them? I suppose you're thieves as well as fools?

ALEXANDER: They're here, sir! *(Holding them up)*

> COREN *goes for the keys but* ALEXANDER *has passed them behind his back.* COREN *goes down the line of pupils.*

COREN: Give me those keys. Come on. This is stupid.

> *He reaches the end of the line to find that they have been passed the other way and the tallest pupil is holding them up and saying 'They're here, sir', but when he tries to get them, they are lobbed over his head to another tall pupil at the other side of the room. The pupils applaud his efforts, but finally he realises that it is hopeless and stands still.*

JACKSON: And in that session of 'Chase the Key', Mr Gerald Coren was knocked out in the first round. Can we have some applause for the loser, please? *(Applause)* Now, what comes next?

CARSWELL: We hadn't finished the quiz on the school rules.

JACKSON: True enough. Back to the desk, sir, for Part Two of our great new quiz game, 'What's That Rule?'

ROSE: I would like to ask if Mr Coren—

SUSAN: Gerald.

ROSE: If Mr Coren actually follows all these rules that he keeps quoting?

KATHERINE: Does he know them all?

GLENYS: Does anybody know them? I don't.

> *There is a general chorus of* 'I don't know 'em', 'Who does?', *etc.*

OLIVE *(taking the rules)*: Right, I'm going to give all of you a test on the school rules. *(General groans)* Sharon, for starters, what is Rule 12?

SHARON: Search me.

CARSWELL: I'll search you, Sharon.

OLIVE: We may have to search *you*, Carswell. Anybody? *(JENNIFER raises her hand.)* Jennifer?

JENNIFER: 'No smoking on the school premises or when representing the school at outside functions.'

OLIVE: Correct! *(Applause)* Yes, Rule 12 forbids smoking. I hope that no one in this class smokes?

ALL: Oo, no, Miss!

OLIVE: Why not, Rose?

ROSE *(reciting)*: Because smoking is a filthy habit, Miss.

YVONNE: It stains the teeth, Miss.

ALISON: And empties the purse, Miss.

SHARON: And rots the lungs, Miss.

ALL: Rots the lungs! *(They cough and gasp.)*

OLIVE *(ringing for silence)*: Quiet. *(To* COREN*)* You, sir: you aren't joining in. I hope you don't smoke?

> JACKSON *pulls a packet of cigarettes out of* COREN's *pocket and holds them up, announcing* 'Mr Coren's *fags!*'

ALL: Aw, Mr Coren!

SUSAN: Naughty Gerald!

OLIVE: Right, next question. *(She hands the rules to* JENNIFER.*)*

JENNIFER: The next question is: 'What is Rule 17?' *(Pause)* Rule 17.

MILSOM: 'No pupil may park a car or motor-bike in the school grounds without permission.'

JENNIFER: Well done! *(Applause)* Yes, as Mrs Ross was pointing out in Assembly only yesterday, the younger generation are getting too lazy. A healthy walk or cycle-ride is much better than sitting slumped in a bus or car. You agree, Mr Coren?

COREN: I suppose so.

JENNIFER: You suppose so. In that case, why do we all see you grind up the drive at five-to-nine every morning in your decrepit Datsun? *(Laughter)* It seems to me that you don't know these rules very well, Mr Coren.

MILSOM: We'd better refresh his memory.

SHARON *(taking the rules)*: Right. Rule 47: 'School dinners provide a balanced meal. The bringing of sandwiches is not encouraged.'

LISTER *(holding up a packet of sandwiches from* COREN*'s case)*: Mr Coren's lunch: one cheese butty, one with brown stuff, one packet of salt-and-vinegar crisps, one Mars bar. *(Laughter)*

SHARON: Rule 9: 'All books must be neatly backed in brown paper.'

JANET *(holding up an unbacked book)*: And here is Mr Coren's notebook, neatly inscribed 'See Diane about Guinness'. *(Laughter)*

YVONNE *(taking the rules)*: Rule 10: 'All lessons must begin on time.' Do Mr Coren's?

ALL: No!

YVONNE: Rule 11: 'All desks must be kept tidy.' Is Mr Coren's?

ALL: No! No!

YVONNE: Rule 33: 'All clothes must be labelled with the owner's name.' Are Mr Coren's? *(Pulling at* COREN*'s collar)*

ALL: No! No! No!

COREN: Stop that! Leave my clothes alone! Those rules are for pupils, not teachers. I'm a grown-up, it's not the same for me.

GLENYS: Why not?

COREN: What?

GLENYS: Why isn't it the same for you?

ALISON: Why can you bring sandwiches and we can't?

ALL: Yeah!

CARSWELL: If smoking's wrong for us, why is it right for you?

ALL: Yeah!

FLETCHER: If we have to listen to what you say, why don't you have to listen to us?

ALL: Yeah!

GOSNEY: We get punished if we get things wrong; why don't you?

ALL: Yeah! *(General hubbub of agreement)*

KATHERINE *(ringing the bell for order)*: I think that you can see now, sir, what it's like to be shouted at and pushed about. Do you like it?

COREN *(after a pause)*: No, I don't. *(The class smile, sigh with relief, etc.)*

HUDSON: So the final question is: 'Are you still going to keep Baldwin in tonight?'

COREN: Of course I am. *(General groans)*

ALEXANDER: What for? He hasn't done anything.

COREN: He was smiling insolently.

All look at BALDWIN, *who is grinning.*

PITCHLEY: He always looks like that, sir, he can't help it. That's why they call him Smiler.

COREN: I still think that he was being insolent. *(General groans)*

JENNIFER: Look, sir. If you keep him in, he'll lose his paper-round. You kept him in last week as well.

BALDWIN *(grinning)*: And I'm saving up for a bike, sir, with my paper-money. And I can join this club next month, sir.

JENNIFER: So imagine what it's like for him, sir. You won't keep him in, will you, sir?

COREN *(after a pause)*: I don't change my mind. I said I'd keep him in, and I will.

Silence

JANET: He's hopeless. What else can we do?

All sit and think.

FLETCHER: Well, talking to him doesn't work, so we'll have to try something drastic.

PITCHLEY: I know! We'll lock him in that little stock-room, and we'll get some glue, and squirt it through the key-hole . . . *(The others grin, shake their heads and say 'No'.)*

LISTER: No! Listen! We go round the back of the school and we get one of those big dustbins. Then we bring it back here and put it over his head . . . Perhaps not.

JANET: Any sensible ideas on how to make Mr Coren a more sensible person?

Another silence.

ELIZABETH: Let's give him a school day.

JANET: What?

ELIZABETH: Give him a school day, like we have. Make him do all the things that we have to do every day.

General agreement.

GLENYS: That is a great idea. Right. Register first. Sit down. I'll be the teacher. You're Coren, right? Sit there.

All sit at their desks. GLENYS sits at the teacher's desk. COREN sits on an empty seat at the front row.

GLENYS: Alexander.
ALEXANDER: Here, Miss.
GLENYS: Baldwin.
BALDWIN: Here, Miss.
GLENYS: Er, Coren. *(Pause)* Coren.
COREN: Here.
GLENYS: Miss.
COREN: Miss.
GLENYS: Here, Miss.
COREN: Here, Miss.
GLENYS: Answer properly next time, Coren . *(A bell sounds.)* Right, line up for Assembly.

All line up. GOSNEY, FLETCHER and HUDSON stand as 'Prefects'. LISTER starts whispering.

GOSNEY *(pushing LISTER)*: You! Shut up!
COREN: Look here –
GOSNEY
FLETCHER } : Shut up! Eyes front! Into the hall!
HUDSON

The class march round the room (to piano accompaniment, if possible) and line up again. COREN is last to arrive.

YVONNE: This morning's reading is from the book of the *Melody Maker*. Here begins this week's Top Ten. *(She reads the current Top Ten in a suitably solemn voice.)* Here ends this morning's reading.

ALISON: This morning's hymn is Number 555, 'All Things Bright And Beautiful', omitting verses 2 to 5.

They sing a verse.

ALISON *(pointing to COREN)*: You. Why didn't you sing?
COREN: I'm not very musical, I'm afraid.
ALISON: That's no excuse. Stay in for singing practice tonight.

A bell rings. They march round again and face the front. Again, COREN is the last to reach his place on the front row.

PITCHLEY *(at the teacher's desk)*: Sit down. General Knowledge. This morning's assembly reading was a short one, and easy to remember. Right. What is this week's Number Three, Carswell?

CARSWELL answers correctly. Applause.

PITCHLEY: Well done. Janet, what is this week's Number Seven?

After some hesitation, JANET answers correctly. Applause.

PITCHLEY: Well done. And now, for the easiest of all, what is this week's Number One? Coren?
COREN: Erm, 'Walking My Baby Back Home'?

Roars of laughter.

PITCHLEY: Tell him, everybody.

All chant the correct answer.

PITCHLEY: Of course. *(To COREN)* You can stay in tonight. That will teach you not to listen in Assembly.

A bell rings.

PITCHLEY: Right. Dismiss.

Again they march round; again COREN is last. (Each march is faster.) ROSE is in the teacher's place.

ROSE: Sit down. Your last English lesson of the week. If you remember, Mrs Ross asked you all to write a piece for the next School Magazine. Take out your work. *(They all do so except* COREN.*)* Make sure your name's on it, then pass it to the front. *(They all do so.)*

ROSE *(to* COREN*)*: You, where's your work? Why haven't you done it?

COREN: I'm the teacher.

ROSE: *What* did you say?

COREN *(shouting)*: I'm the teacher!

ROSE: Dearie me! That's no excuse for shouting and not doing your homework. Write it out three times for Monday. *(A bell rings.)* Stand up. Off you go.

They march round, this time at a frenetic pace, leaving COREN *even later than usual.* JANET *is the teacher.*

JANET: Sit down quietly. *(They sit noisily.)* Stand up! Now this time sit quietly. *(They do.)* That's better. Your final Maths lesson of the week. A bit of football league table revision first. Here's the problem. Near the end of the season, four teams are in danger of relegation. Team A has played 39 games, winning 9 and drawing 11; Team B has also played 39, winning 8 and drawing 13; Team C has played 40, winning 10 and drawing 8, while Team D has only played 36, winning 7 and drawing 12. Among the remaining fixtures, Team A has to play Team B. And remember, it's 3 points for a win. Now the problem is, how many points does Team D have to score in its remaining matches to be sure of avoiding relegation?

All heads go down, and hands start to go up, until everyone's is raised except COREN's.

JANET: Come on, Gerald, you're always last, aren't you? *(His hand goes up.)* Well?

COREN: 10 points. *(Laughter from the class)*

JANET: Olive?

OLIVE: Miss, 14 points.

JANET: Correct. Who else got 14? *(All hands go up.)* Well done!

Gerald Coren, you'll have to stay in tonight and do 20 more examples.

   COREN *sits slumped in his place.*

BALDWIN: Do you see what it's like, sir? Teachers keep you in for things you just can't do, even if you try your best. How would you like to have to do 20 more examples like that?

GOSNEY: One, two, three, four . . . *(The rest of the class join in until they reach 20 in a shout.)*

COREN *(screaming)*: Stop it! *(He sits with his head in his arms. Pause)*

CARSWELL: We'll have Rugby next. You'll enjoy that, sir.

SHARON: Leave him alone now.

CARSWELL: You want to play, don't you, sir? Rugby's good fun.

COREN: I'd rather play Soccer.

CARSWELL: Oo, you shouldn't say that, sir. Mr Tate was telling us yesterday that every real English chap prefers Rugby. He says that Soccer is for hooligans.

GOSNEY: Yeah. Let's have tackling practice; we'll practise on Sir.

FLETCHER: Great idea! Line up, lads.

   The BOYS *line up in front of the desks.*

GOSNEY: Come on, Gerald, run the gauntlet.

COREN: It will soon be half-past three, and then you will be punished.

GOSNEY: If you don't run, we'll make you.

   A boy near COREN *tries to push him.*

COREN: Leave me alone! I'm a human being!

JACKSON: Oh! I'm a bean!

KAYE: I'm a baked bean!

LISTER: And I'm a runner bean!

MILSOM: I'm a Crosse and Blackwell bean!

HUDSON: And soon Sir will be a has-been! Come on.

As some of the BOYS *start to close on* COREN, SHARON *suddenly comes forward.*

SHARON: Leave him alone, you bullies!

Most of the GIRLS *form a barrier round the teacher's desk, chanting* 'Get back!' *to the others, who retreat grinning to the back of the room.*

EGGSWORTH *(picking up an exercise-book)*: Hey, hand-grenade!

He lobs the book towards COREN, *others do the same and the* GIRLS *try to field them.*

GIRLS: Leave him alone! Get off him! You'll hurt him! How would you like it! Wait till I get you!

The others are jeering and laughing. The noise reaches a climax. OLIVE *jumps on a desk ringing the bell.*

OLIVE: Stop it! Stop it!

Silence.

OLIVE: We're being worse than he is! What were we supposed to be doing? Showing him how he treats us. But he doesn't turn our desks over and push us about and open our bags and throw things at us. What good are we doing? We're just going to make him worse. Look how upset he is. *(A bell rings.)* That's first bell; five minutes to home time. Sit down and leave him alone.

They drift back to their places and look at COREN, *still slumped in despair.*

DEBRA: You came here straight from college, didn't you, sir? *(*COREN *nods.)*

ALISON: I bet you're only about 22, aren't you, sir? *(*COREN *nods. Murmurs from the class)*

MILSOM: I wouldn't like to have to teach us lot if I'd just left college.

KAYE: I wouldn't like to teach us lot at all.

JACKSON: I wouldn't like to teach anybody anything.

Laughter

ELIZABETH: I suppose teaching's a bit hard when you're just starting, isn't it, sir? *(COREN nods.)*

GOSNEY: How is it hard? You're talking daft.

ELIZABETH: Shut it, bird–brain.

ROSE: We've been a bit unfair to him really. *(Murmurs of agreement)*

ROSE: We're not a bad lot, you know, sir, but you have been a bit strict sometimes. Like, Debra's mother wouldn't give her time to learn any poetry last night, but you wouldn't listen to her, would you? I expect you've got your own troubles, haven't you, sir?

KATHERINE: Everybody has.

BALDWIN: Your wife's been in hospital, hasn't she, sir? My auntie told me. *(COREN nods.)*

GIRLS: Aw!

BALDWIN *(half-whispering to the class)*: She's had a baby.

Further 'Aw's from the GIRLS and grins from the BOYS. ROSE and KATHERINE whisper, then hurry round the class saying 'Collection for Sir'.

COREN *(raising his head)*: Have we finished? We seem to have done just about every subject.

KAYE: We didn't have a music–lesson. *(Moans from some of the class)* Well, it's the only lesson I like.

LISTER: Fair enough. We've just time for Sir's favourite tune. What's your favourite, sir?

COREN: Silence.

LISTER: Silence is not actually a tune, Mr Coren.

OLIVE: It is! It's here somewhere. *(She looks through the cupboard.)*

JENNIFER: Let's tidy up while we listen.

OLIVE puts on 'The Sound Of Silence'. The class finish tidying up, then listen to the music.

KAYE: Hi, sir.

JACKSON: Good old sir.

SHARON: Super sir.

BALDWIN: Have a sweet, sir? *(They smile at him.)*

COREN: Thank you.

KAYE: And a crisp, sir?

COREN *(with a faint smile)*: Ta.

HUDSON: Drink of pop, sir?

GOSNEY: Cigar, sir? *(Laughter)*

COREN *(smiling)*: No, thank you.

KATHERINE *(coming forward)*: Sir, we would like to apologise
for upsetting you, and we should like you to buy something for
your new baby. *(She tips the money onto the desk.)* Three pounds
32½p, sir, 2 pesetas and some chocolate buttons.

Laughter. COREN *joins in. The bell rings.* COREN *switches the
record off.*

COREN *(to* BALDWIN*)*: Well, Andrew, it's time for your paper-
round.

BALDWIN *(grinning)*: Yes, sir.

COREN: I don't suppose any of you feel like doing any
homework this week-end?

ALL: No, sir.

COREN: Quite right. I think we all deserve a rest. Would you
unlock the door please, Paul? *(*ALEXANDER *unlocks the door.)*
Thank you.

ALEXANDER: Your keys, sir.

COREN: Thank you. Oh, I'd forgotten, if I cancel your lines,
will you cancel mine?

ALL: Yes, sir.

COREN: Thank you. And thanks for the lesson, though I think
we'll have a quieter one on Monday.

SUSAN: Can we go a minute early for a treat, sir?

COREN: Well, the school rules say –

ALL: Ah ah!

COREN: All right, but don't run.

> BALDWIN *races out. There is a shout in the corridor: 'Andrew Baldwin, come here'. The class laugh and troop out, saying good night.* COREN *gets his things together.*

DEBRA *(last out, by the desk)*: Is your wife out of hospital now, sir? *(*COREN *nods.)* You'll be wanting to get home to her.
COREN: And you'll be wanting to get home to your mother.
DEBRA: Aw, her. Well, she's not all that bad. Sometimes she's awkward, but sometimes she's nice.
COREN: Like all of us. Off you go. Good night, Debra.
DEBRA: 'Night, sir. *(Exit)*

> *The bell rings.* MRS ROSS *enters.*

MRS ROSS: I was teaching next door. I nearly came in, but I didn't know if you needed any help.
COREN: I did, but I got it from the class. It was a good lesson, really.
MRS ROSS: Oh. Have a good week-end.
COREN: And you. *(Exit* MRS ROSS*)*

> COREN *looks after her for a moment, looks at the rules, tears them up and drops them in the waste-bin. He gathers his things, goes to the door, looks round, and switches off the light. The door slams.*

CURTAIN

ROBBY NUDD

CHARACTERS

ROBBY NUDD
LITTLE JOHN
WILL SCARLETT
ALAN-A-DALE
THOMAS
SMALLEST OUTLAW
FRIAR TUCK
  (*Robby's mother in disguise*)
MARIAN
BIG BRIDGET
DEBORAH
JANE
SHIRLEY

GLENDA
CHRISTINE
SHERIFF OF NOTTINGHAM
FIRST DEPUTY
SECOND DEPUTY
THIRD DEPUTY
FOURTH DEPUTY
STALLHOLDER 1 *(sweetmeats)*
STALLHOLDER 2 *(apples)*
STALLHOLDER 3 *(peaches)*
STALLHOLDER 4 *(pies)*
CITIZENS

SCENE 1: Sherbert Forest
SCENE 2: A busy market day in Nottingham

NOTE ON STAGING

If your stage has a traverse curtain, the market stalls for Scene 2 can be set up ready behind it. Otherwise, Robby's gang can take the 'Sherbert Forest' sign as they go off, while the stallholders and citizens carry on their stalls as they shout the first lines of Scene 2.

PROPERTIES

Scene 1
Bows, arrows, comics (GANG)
Bag of easy-to-eat sweets (FRIAR)

Scene 2
Shopping bags (DEBORAH's with woolly animal) (GIRLS)
Two guns (SHERIFF)
Gun, box/bag 'Test 1' with woolly rabbit (DEPUTY 1)
Gun, eight extra stars (DEPUTY 2)
Gun, bags labelled 'Gold' and 'Silver' (DEPUTY 3)
Gun, rod with cord and watch (DEPUTY 4)
Bow and arrows (with suckers for safety) (ROBBY)

SOUND EFFECTS

Whistle, bell, drum-roll, shots, horses' hooves.

ROBBY NUDD

SCENE 1: *A sign says 'Sherbert Forest'. ROBBY's gang are lazing around, mending bows and reading comics. WILL is examining a toadstool.*

Their clothes are a mixture of modern and traditional. Enter LITTLE JOHN

JOHN: On your feet, lads. Give us a smile and off we go.

They smile and face the audience.

JOHN: This is the tale of Robert Nudd,
        (His friends all call him Robby.)
WILL: And he was born in Nottingham.
ALAN: His father was a bobby.
FRIAR: Young Robby wished to follow Dad –
        He too would join the fuzz.
THOMAS: But they said 'You're just not tall enough'
SMALLEST OUTLAW: So he joined up with us.
ALL: Now we are the men of the greenwood.
        This forest where we is
        Is known as Sherbert Forest
        Cos it's full of fun and fizz. Hey!

They end with arms extended and happy smiles. Slowly they droop and look sad.

ALAN: Well, that's a laugh for a start. When did we last have any fun in this forest?
WILL: Oh, I think it's good here, Alan. I like the trees and the

bees and the toadstools.

ALAN: What's good about them, Will Scarlett? There's not much fun in fungus.

THOMAS: No. And another thing, we're supposed to be robbers, aren't we?

ALL: Yeah!

THOMAS: Well, when did we last rob anybody?

FRIAR: Er, we robbed that old woman last Thursday.

JOHN: Aw, come on, Friar, what did we get? A spare pair of false teeth and a pension book. She hadn't any food, not even a packet of Polos. And I'm starving.

ALAN: Aren't we all? And the food's got worse since Robby brought the girls in to do the cooking.

All moan and nod.

SMALLEST: And I'm always cold. Let me keep warm under your robe, Friar.

He tries to get under FRIAR's *robe while the others laugh.* FRIAR *pushes him away.*

FRIAR: Get off! Quiet, here comes Robby.

Enter ROBBY.

JOHN: Attention!

The GANG *shuffle into line.*

ROBBY: Morning, Little John. Morning, men.

GANG: Morning, Robby.

ROBBY: Any problems?

THOMAS: Yes. Look, Robby, sir, when are we going to rob anybody? We're tired of just sitting around here.

SMALLEST: And we're hungry and cold as well, sir. I think we should –

ROBBY: Quiet. I'll do the thinking round here. I'm your leader, and –

MARIAN *(off)*: Robby! Robby! *(She enters.)* Oh, there you are.

ROBBY: What do you want now, Marian? And why ⌐
yelling like that?

MARIAN: I'm yelling because it's the only way to get anyon⌐
listen in this forest of yours. Now what do you and the other⌐
want to eat today?

ROBBY: Oh, give us what you want. Who cares?

MARIAN: I care, and the other girls care. Say what you want and
we will cook it.

ALAN: It'll be a change if you do cook it. That meat stuff
yesterday was half-raw.

MARIAN: Half-raw!

The other OUTLAWS *mutter agreement.*

JOHN: Yes, it was. What was it, anyway?

MARIAN: That was fried toad. I thought it went down a treat.

ALAN: It came up a treat as well.

The others laugh.

MARIAN: Right. That settles it. *(shouting)* Come here, girls.

The GIRLS *march in. They also wear a mixture of modern and
mediaeval dress, including aprons with their names on. They fold their
arms, looking angry.*

SHIRLEY: What's the matter, Marian?

MARIAN: Food is the matter. I'm getting the usual insults.

ROBBY: What do you girls think that you're doing here? You're
supposed to be cooking.

SHIRLEY: And what are we supposed to cook, eh?

BRIDGET: There isn't any point in cooking because you criticise
everything we make. All of you, even him. *(Pointing at smallest
outlaw)*

SMALLEST: Well, all your food tastes the same. *(The* GANG
agree.)

MARIAN: The same! We've varied our menus every day to try
and please you. What have we had this last week, girls?

JANE: Monday it was fried nut cutlets. Walnuts.

111

ALAN: Walnuts! I found a piece of stone in mine.

WILL: It must have been a piece of the wall. *(GANG laugh.)*

JANE: Oh, very witty.

DEBORAH: Tuesday it was fried hedgehog. And don't you dare say that you found a piece of hedge in it, Alan-a-Dale, or I'll thump you.

ROBBY: Steady on, Deborah, that's not very ladylike. Look, girls, we all know that you're doing your best under difficult conditions, but you must admit that the food is rather monotonous. For one thing, it's always fried, isn't it?

JOHN: We've actually written a song about your fried food. Would you like to hear it?

MARIAN: I don't suppose we've much choice. Go ahead.

JOHN: It's called 'Every Day Is Friday In The Forest'.

GANG: We've got a little problem in the forest,
And we've got to look that problem in the eye.
Every day is Friday in the forest
'Cos the girls have only learned to fry.

For breakfast Mother's Pride is fried with bacon,
For lunch it's nearly always fish.
For tea, although it's after change we're achin',
We get another fried-up dish.

We've urged the girls to modify their menus,
We've pressured them from every side.

MARIAN: We once went out and bought you forty Mars bars.

SMALLEST *(to audience)*: Have you ever had Mars bars fried?

GANG: Yeuch!

(They repeat the first verse.)

MARIAN: Thank you very much, that was very encouraging.

WILL: No, but seriously, girls, there are so many other ways to cook as well as frying. For instance, that toad yesterday could have been so much better if you'd simply mixed together some mustard, vinegar, wine, soy sauce, rosemary, ginger, seasoning –

ALAN: And garlic.

WILL: And garlic, yes.

THOMAS: And poured it over the toad.

JOHN: And allowed it to marinate for several hours.

GANG: That's right.

(They nod and smile.)

SHIRLEY: And where are we supposed to get all that stuff from?
  You don't help, sitting about.

GLENDA: Anyway, frying's the only way we can cook, see?

CHRISTINE: Yeah, we didn't like cookery at school; it was
  boring.

MARIAN: And it's all very well you mocking us, but at least we
  are doing something, which is more than I can say for you lot.

JANE: Yes, why don't you go and steal something from a farm?
  That would help.

GLENDA: Or rob some travellers of their money.

CHRISTINE: Yeah, you're supposed to be robbers.

WILL: I don't like robbing.

ROBBY: Watch it, Will Scarlett!

WILL: No, I don't mean you, Robin. I mean I don't like robbing
  people.

ROBBY: But who else is there to rob?

JOHN: Stop arguing! There won't be anyone to rob today
  because everyone's in Nottingham for the fair.

ROBBY: You're right, John. We'll start robbing again next week.

BRIDGET: You're making excuses again. If you're scared of
  robbing people, give us your weapons and we'll rob 'em.

SHIRLEY: Yes, we can't do any worse than you.

DEBORAH: And if you don't like our cooking, *you* can do it for
  a change.

SMALLEST: What are you talking about? Cooking's a woman's
  job. It takes a real man to be a robber.

BRIDGET: That lets you out then, doesn't it, sunshine? *(Pushing
  him.)*

MARIAN: Leave him alone, Bridget. It's just not good enough,

113

Robin. We came to the forest because you said it was fun,
   didn't we, girls?

GIRLS: That's right. We did.

MARIAN: Well, it's not fun for us. Cooking all the time is boring.
   And we never get any thanks for it, you just insult us. Cooking
   for you lot makes us sick.

ALAN: It makes us sick as well.

   GANG *laugh and mime being sick.*

MARIAN: That's the last straw! We try to discuss things and all
   you can do is mock us. Are we taking any more of it, girls?

GIRLS: No! *(They take their aprons off.)*

ROBBY: Ey, what are you going to do now?

BRIDGET: We're going back to Nottingham. You'll need aprons
   if you have to cook for yourselves.

ROBBY: Oh, come on, be reasonable. Give us a chance. We'll go
   now and steal some money at Nottingham Fair to buy you
   what you need.

MARIAN: Good. We'll see you there. Come on, girls. *(The*
   GIRLS *start to move off.)*

THOMAS: We'll get you anything you want.

JANE: You know what you can get, Thomas?

THOMAS: Tell me.

GIRLS: Get lost! *(They blow raspberries and exeunt. Pause)*

WILL: What do we do now, Robin?

ROBBY: Oh, we'll manage without them.

FRIAR: Have a sweet, Robin? *(*ROBBY *takes a sweet from a bag that*
   FRIAR TUCK *offers him.)*

ROBBY: Thanks, Friar.

WILL: You mean *you'll* manage without them, you and the Friar.
   You two always have enough to eat, don't you?

SMALLEST: I've noticed that. Friar always has sweets.

ALAN: Yes, and you only share them with Robin. Why?

FRIAR: Because he's our leader. He needs extra nourishment so
   that he can think and plan for all of us.

GANG: Is that so?

FRIAR
ROBBY } : Yes, it is.

JOHN: Well, what have you planned? We've got no money and no food, and the girls have just walked out, so what are we going to do?

GANG: Yeah. Right. You tell him, Little John.

SMALLEST: What's the plan, Robin, sir?

ROBBY: Er, I'm not quite sure. *(Groans from the GANG)* There are hardly any travellers to rob, and we've got no money of our own to buy food. What *can* we do?

FRIAR: What about looking for other jobs?

THOMAS: Who's going to give us a job? We're only trained to work as outlaws, to do things like robbing people and using our bows and arrows.

ROBBY: Using our bows and arrows! That's right, Thomas. Listen, everybody: there's always an archery contest at Nottingham Fair, right? *(They nod.)* and the prize is a bag of gold. If I can win that, we can buy as much food as we want, and get the girls to come back with us. *(Applause from the others)*

FRIAR: Good thinking, Robby. Have another sweet.

ROBBY: Oh, thanks, Friar.

JOHN: Wait a minute. If we go to Nottingham the Sheriff'll arrest us, won't he?

SMALLEST: If he tries to arrest me, I'll just have to kill him.

ALAN: You joking? Him and his deputies have all got guns.

SMALLEST: Then why don't we go in disguise?

ALAN: That's right. You could go as a garden gnome.

ROBBY: No, disguise is a great idea, little 'un. Look, the girls have left their aprons. We'll put 'em on and disguise ourselves as women.

JOHN: It's a risk, but it just might work. Shall we try it, lads?

GANG: Yeah, all right.

ROBBY: Right, men, grab an apron. Off we go to Nottingham. When we return, we'll be rich *and* we'll have had a good meal. Mmm, I can smell those hot meat pies already.

The GANG exeunt chattering excitedly.

SCENE 2: *A busy market day in Nottingham.*

STALLHOLDER 1: Buy our sweetmeats. Buy our Nottingham rock. Take a stick home for the kids. Buy your sweets here.

STALLHOLDER 2: English apples, crisp and juicy. Eat 'em or bake 'em. They're lovely.

STALLHOLDER 3: Peaches. Peaches. Peaches. Get your peaches here. Only one penny per pound. Peaches. Peaches.

STALLHOLDER 4: Hot pies. Pies. Hot pies. You can't resist 'em. Hot from the oven. Hot pies. Hot pies.

Enter all the girls except MARIAN.

DEBORAH: Where's Marian gone?

BRIDGET: She stopped to buy a present for Robby.

SHIRLEY: I know what I'd give him, and it wouldn't be a present.

JANE: Oh, forget him. Let's look round the stalls.

The GIRLS *wander round the stalls as the* STALLHOLDERS *shout again. Shots are heard. All heads turn.*

CHRISTINE: Who's that firing guns?

STALLHOLDER 1: It's probably the Sheriff and his men.

GLENDA: Who's he shooting at?

STALLHOLDER 2: Could be anybody. He just shoots folk for fun.

DEBORAH: Ooh, that's awful! Why is he so nasty?

All listen.

STALLHOLDER 1: They say his wife left him and he had a – He's here.

Noise of horses' hooves. SHERIFF *and* DEPUTIES *rush in. They wear cowboy costumes, with stars and revolvers. The Sheriff's star is very big. The* CROWD *mutter.*

SHERIFF: Quiet! Now I am the Sheriff of Nottingham
        And the peasants are scared of my gun.

I'm getting so skilful at potting 'em
That I often just shoot one for fun. Bang!

He shoots several shots at the feet of a STALLHOLDER *who
shrieks and dances. The* SHERIFF *laughs.*

SHERIFF *(to his* DEPUTIES*)*: Gather round, men. They say
Robby Nudd means to come into town today, and I want him
captured alive.

DEPUTY 1: Why don't we kill him, Sheriff, like that bloke last
week?

DEPUTY 2: Yeah, Robby's tried to kill us before now.

DEPUTY 3: Besides, what's the good of being a lawman if you
can't kill criminals?

DEPUTY 4: Yeah, killing people is fun.

OTHERS: Yeah. That's right.

SHERIFF: Shut up! I want Robby Nudd alive, for reasons of my
own. I'm going to make an announcement now. *(To the*
CROWD*)* Are you all listening?

CROWD: Oh, ar, yes, we be listening, *etc.*

SHERIFF *(to the* DEPUTIES*)*: Get the rabble quiet.

DEPUTIES *draw guns and threaten the* CROWD.

SHERIFF: Good. Now listen, you pathetic peasants. Today is the
day of the great fair.

STALLHOLDER 1: Yes, it is.

SHERIFF: Shut it! Today is the day of the great fair, and coming
into Nottingham will be many strangers.

ALL: Strangers!

SHERIFF: Yes, and among those strangers will be the dreaded
outlaw, Robby Nudd.

ALL: Robby Nudd!

SHERIFF: Yes. Now, for anyone who gives information leading
to his arrest, there is a reward.

ALL: A reward!

SHERIFF: Stop repeating what I say. Show 'em the reward.
*(*DEPUTY 3 *holds up a bag labelled 'Silver'. 'Ooh's from the*

CROWD*)* Yes! a bag of silver for whoever finds him. And remember, Nudd is a master of disguise. He may come dressed as a friar, or a tramp, or even as a woman.

STALLHOLDER 3: How shall we know if he be not a proper woman, Sheriff?

SHERIFF: Who said that? *(STALLHOLDER 3 raises a shaking hand.)* Do you want my boys to burn your miserable stall to the ground? *(STALLHOLDER 3 shakes her head.)* Then be quiet when I'm talking. Now, you may wonder how you'll know if he be not a woman. Well, we have a test to administer to doubtful characters, and my deputy here will show you how it works. *(To DEPUTY 1)* Show 'em, boy.

DEPUTY 1 *(holding up a box labelled 'Test 1')*: This test has been devised by famous scientists from Nottingham University. It is 99 per cent accurate. Come here, you, and you, lady. *(He beckons DEPUTY 2 and STALLHOLDER 1.)* Stand there please, and there. *(He stands one on each side of him.)* Both close your eyes till I tell you. *(They do so.)* Observe, everybody. *(He holds up a toy rabbit. The CROWD mutter excitedly.)* Quiet please. Jake, open your eyes. *(He shows him the rabbit.)* Now, what do you say? *(A bell rings.)*

DEPUTY 2: Er, it's a rabbit.

DEPUTY 1: Correct, it's a rabbit! *(Applause)*

STALLHOLDER 4: Well, what does that prove?

DEPUTY 1: Just watch. Now, madam, open your eyes. What do you say? *(A bell rings.)*

STALLHOLDER 1: Aw, isn't it lovely?

DEPUTY 1: Which proves that you are female. I believe that you *are* female, madam?

STALLHOLDER 1: That is correct. *(Applause)*

DEPUTY 1: It works every time, ladies and gentlemen. Show a lady the rabbit and she will say 'Aw, isn't it lovely'. Look! *(He shows the rabbit to STALLHOLDER 3.)*

STALLHOLDER 3: Aw, isn't it lovely? *(Laughter)*

SHERIFF: So all is ready for Robby Nudd, whether he comes in disguise or not. I have scouts ready to signal if a stranger approaches. *(A whistle sounds.)* Hark! Someone is coming. It could be Robby Nudd. Get ready, men.

The DEPUTIES *mingle with the crowd. Silence. All watch the entrance. Enter* MARIAN, *wearing a hood.*

STALLHOLDER 3 *(pointing)*: That is Robby Nudd! I claim the reward!

SHERIFF: Seize him! *(*DEPUTIES *seize* MARIAN.*)*

DEPUTY 2: I arrest you as the notorious outlaw, Robby Nudd.

MARIAN: I am only a woman.

DEPUTY 2: We've only your word for that.

STALLHOLDER 3: It's Robby Nudd. Give me the money!

MARIAN: Unhand me!

SHERIFF: Stop! Administer the test.

MARIAN: What test? Don't be cheeky.

DEPUTY 1: Silence, man.

MARIAN: Woman.

DEPUTY 1: Or woman. Now, are you ready?

MARIAN: I don't know.

DEPUTY 1: Say 'Yes'.

MARIAN: Yes.

DEPUTY 1: Good. Close your eyes. You have nothing to fear if you are innocent.

He produces the rabbit. Drum roll.

DEPUTY 1: Open your eyes. *(Bell rings.)*

MARIAN: Aw, isn't it lovely?

DEPUTY 1: You are a woman!

MARIAN: That's right. *(Applause)*

SHERIFF: I am sorry for any inconvenience, miss. You are free to go. *(*CROWD *applaud. To* STALLHOLDER 3*)* Better luck next time, madam. *(To the crowd)* Be on your guard, good folks. Come, men.

Exeunt SHERIFF *and* DEPUTIES. *The other* GIRLS *crowd round* MARIAN. ROBBY *and the* GANG *sidle on badly disguised as women, all wearing aprons.* ROBBY *hides his bow and arrows by a stall.*

MARIAN: What's all this testing about?

GLENDA: The Sheriff says Robby is coming to town disguised as a woman. *(ROBBY and the GANG stop and listen.)*

CHRISTINE: Yes, they show you this rabbit, and if you're a woman you say 'Aw, isn't it lovely?' *(ROBBY and the GANG turn to each other and mouth 'Aw, isn't it lovely'.)*

DEBORAH: Do you think the others will come with him?

JANE: Probably. We'd better keep out of their way. I bet they're still in a bad mood.

BRIDGET: Forget 'em. Let's get our shopping done.

MARIAN: Have you bought anything yet?

DEBORAH: Oh, yes. Look what I've bought. *(She takes a woolly animal from her bag.)*

GIRLS: Aw, isn't it lovely?

The GIRLS laugh and go out chattering. The STALLHOLDERS start their cries again. The GANG begin to sniff the air and cluster round the pie stall.

STALLHOLDER 4: Hot pies! Hot pies! Eat 'em while they're hot! They're lovely! Now then, er, gents –

JOHN: Ladies.

STALLHOLDER 4: Er, ladies. Now then, ladies, can I tempt you to buy a succulent hot pie, dripping with gravy and goodness? You won't find a better pie in the kingdom.

SMALLEST: How much do they cost?

STALLHOLDER 4: 1p per pie.

SMALLEST: Peeperpie?

STALLHOLDER 4: 1p per pie, or 1p per peas, or 2p per pie and per peas.

WILL: Oh. Well, they smell lovely, but we've no money, I'm afraid. You see, we're out – er, out-of-work.

Shots off-stage. Horse hooves. SHERIFF *and* DEPUTIES *race in with guns drawn.*

SHERIFF: Well, has anyone seen Robby Nudd yet?
ALL: No, Sheriff.

SHERIFF *walks slowly round till he comes to* ROBBY.

SHERIFF *(To* ROBBY*)*: You, have you seen him?
ROBBY: No, I haven't seen him. Never. Not me. No.
GANG: We haven't either. Not us. No.
DEPUTY 2: Wait a minute. You're not women. You're men.
ALAN: We're women. Look at our aprons.
DEPUTY 2: Fair enough. *(He inspects them.)* What's your name?
THOMAS *(Looking at apron which says 'Deborah')*: Er, Harobed.
DEPUTY 2: What?
THOMAS: Aw, I mean Deborah. Deborah.
DEPUTY 3: I don't trust them.
DEPUTY 4: Let's shoot 'em.
DEPUTY 1: Good idea! *(They draw their guns.)*
ROBBY: Wait! Give us the test.
SHERIFF: Oh, all right. Give 'em the test.

Immediately the GANG *line up and as* DEPUTY 1 *takes out the rabbit, all chant 'Aw, isn't it lovely?'*

SHERIFF: What?
GANG: Aw, isn't it lovely?

Everyone stares at DEPUTY 1 *who shrugs.*

DEPUTY 1: They're women all right, Sheriff. The test has proved it. *(The* GANG *all grin.)*
SHERIFF: You and your test. Come on, we'll find Robby Nudd yet.

Exeunt SHERIFF *and* DEPUTIES.

WILL: Phew! We were lucky that time, Robby.
STALLHOLDER 4: Ladies! Ladies! I must get rid of these pies today. If you've no money, what about a barter?
FRIAR: What's a barter?

STALLHOLDER 4: Barter means you give me something instead of money for my pies.

JOHN: We haven't anything, have we, lads? I mean, laddies, er, ladies?

WILL: Wait a minute! We've a bow and arrows hidden over there.

STALLHOLDER 4:What?

ROBBY *(cuffing* WILL *and smiling at* STALLHOLDER 4*)*: She said 'We've a row of marrows near the midden over there'. But they're not ripe yet.

STALLHOLDER 4: Well, if you've nothing to barter, it's no good.

ALAN: I've an idea! What about our aprons?

GANG: Yes!

ALAN: Will you take those?

STALLHOLDER 4: I will indeed; they look very good aprons. I'll give you a pie each for just two aprons.

ROBBY: You're on! *(He and* ALAN *start to remove their aprons.)*

STALLHOLDER 1: Get your sweetmeats here! Nottingham rock, one stick per apron!

STALLHOLDER 2: Don't forget your apples! Crisp and juicy! One pound per apron.

STALLHOLDER 3: Lovely peaches! Two pounds per one apron.

The GANG *remove their aprons and begin to barter when the* SHERIFF *and* DEPUTIES *reappear and start to cross the stage.*

STALLHOLDER 1: Hey, Sheriff, what about the archery contest?

OTHERS: Yeah, what about it?

SHERIFF: Shut your mouths, you common peasants. I'll decide when we have the archery contest. We, er, we'll have it *now*. Announce it, you. *(To* DEPUTY 3*)*

DEPUTY 3: Hear ye, hear ye. *(The* GIRLS *enter.)* Come in, if you're coming. The great archery contest is about to begin, sponsored jointly by Nottingham's manufacturers: John Player, Jesse Boot, and, of course, Sturmey Archer. Any man may enter this contest. The first prize is one bag of gold. Each contestant will take one shot at the target over there. *(He gestures to the wings.)* An outer will be signalled by one bell. *(One bell rings.)* An inner will be signalled by two bells. *(Two bells ring.)* And a bull's eye will be signalled by three bells. *(Three bells ring.)* As usual, the Sheriff will fire the first shot. If you would be so kind, Sheriff? *(The* SHERIFF *aims and shoots. All watch the arrow. A shriek from offstage)* And the Sheriff has hit an innocent bystander! *(Applause)* Now, may we have the next contestant please? *(*ROBBY *steps forward carrying a bow and arrow. Cheers from the* CROWD*)* Your name and address?

ROBBY: Er, Greenwood.

DEPUTY 3: Is that your name or your address?

ROBBY: Er, both.

DEPUTY 3: Oh. Well, you know the rules? *(*ROBBY *nods.)* Right. Take aim. Shoot!

> ROBBY *shoots. All watch the arrow through the air. Two bells sound.*

DEPUTY 3: An inner! Two points! *(Applause)* Next contestant please. *(There is silence.)* This is unusual. Is there nobody else? In that case, the prize goes to our second contestant –

MARIAN: Stop! I wish to enter.

ROBBY: You!

MARIAN: Yes, me, Mr Greenwood. I am a qualified archer. Give me a bow and arrow. *(*ROBBY *glumly hands them over.)*

DEPUTY 3: Your name please?

MARIAN: Er, Cook.

DEPUTY 3: Address?

MARIAN *(showing her dress)*: How about this one?

DEPUTY 3: Very nice. You know the rules? *(*MARIAN *nods.)* Right. Take aim. Shoot!

> MARIAN *shoots. All watch the arrow through the air. Three bells sound.*

DEPUTY 3: A bull's eye! Three points! *(Applause)* Are there any more contestants? *(Pause)* In that case, I proclaim that the winner is the third contestant, who wins the bag of gold!

ROBBY: Wait! I protest! It is written in the rules that no woman may win this prize, so I am the winner.

Uproar among the crowd.

SHERIFF: Quiet! But you and these others also claim to be women, do you not?

ROBBY: What? *(Remembering, and speaking in a high-pitched voice)* Oh yes, I am a woman, I am, yes.

GANG *(also high-pitched)*: I'm a woman. I'm not a man. Aw, isn't it lovely?

SHERIFF: Quiet!!

All are instantly silent except for LITTLE JOHN, *who is standing, eyes closed, talking in a loud, high voice.*

JOHN: Oh. I agree. Men just don't realise all the problems that we women have, like finding the right shampoo, and then tights – Aren't tights a problem? *(He opens his eyes to find that everyone is staring at him. He gives a sickly smile and flutters a little wave at the* SHERIFF.*)*

SHERIFF: A woman! Huh! You're a man. You're all men, and one of you is Robby Nudd. You, what's your real name?

ROBBY: Rob–er, Robin–, er, Robinetta.

SHERIFF: You have a beard, Robinetta.

ROBBY: It's er, it's embarrassing non–feminine facial hair. I'm trying to get rid of it.

SHERIFF: You think I believe that? Give 'em all the second test. *(The* DEPUTIES *gasp.)*

DEPUTY 4: Not the second test, Chief!

SHERIFF: And why not?

DEPUTY 4: We don't know if it's safe. It's only been tried on guinea–pigs.

SHERIFF: Get it. Somebody as well as guinea–pigs has to suffer. I hope you all agree? *(The* GANG *all nod.)* Good. Carry on. Stand in a line, you so–called women. *(They do so.)*

DEPUTY 4: Watch carefully, please.

He produces a rod with a cord attached to one end. On the end of the cord is a large watch. DEPUTY 4 *stands behind the* GANG. *The* CROWD *murmur excitedly.*

DEPUTY 4: Quiet, please. This is a lie–detector test and may or may not cause permanent mental harm. *(To the* GANG*)* All you have to do is watch the watch and repeat the words 'Watch the watch'. Are you ready? *(The* GANG *nod.)* Good. Everyone else can help by repeating the words. Off we go.

He swings the watch across in front of the GANG, *who follow it with their heads while everyone chants* 'Watch the watch'. *Gradually the watch stops with the* GANG *staring fixedly at it.*

DEPUTY 4: Sh! Now they are hypnotised and they can only speak the truth. Observe. The rabbit, please.

DEPUTY 4 *walks down the line of* OUTLAWS *and shows each the rabbit. Each in turn says* 'It's a rabbit' *in a drugged voice and* DEPUTY 4 *announces* 'A man!' *while the* CROWD *exclaims. The last outlaw in the line is* FRIAR TUCK.

FRIAR: Aw, isn't it lovely?
DEPUTY 4: Man! *(Doubletake)* What?
FRIAR: Aw, isn't it lovely?
DEPUTY 4: This one's a woman!
ALL: A woman!
FRIAR *(throwing back her hood)*: Yes! I am a woman! *(Applause)* *(The* GANG *blink and look round.)* My name is Nelly Nudd!
ALL: Nelly Nudd!
FRIAR: Yes! I am Robby's mother!
ALL: His mother!
ROBBY *(running and embracing her)*: Mother!
ALL: Robby Nudd! *(Applause)*
DEPUTY 4: But why are you in disguise, Mrs Nudd?
FRIAR: I disguised myself so that I could follow my boy to the forest and look after him and give him sweets and make sure that he had a clean handkerchief every day.
STALLHOLDER 3: Well done, Mrs Nudd! *(Applause)*

ROBBY: But what has happened to my father? Where is he now?

FRIAR: Your father is here! *(General amazement)* He is now *(pause)* – the Sheriff of Nottingham!

SHERIFF *(embracing her)*: Nelly! My wife!

FRIAR: Horace! My husband!

BOTH *(embracing ROBBY)*: Robby! Our son! *(Applause)*

FRIAR: You won't go back in that nasty forest, and be an outlaw again, will you, son?

ROBBY: I must go back, Mother. It's the only trade I know. I wanted to be a lawman like my dad, but I am too small.

SHERIFF: You're not too small now, son.

ROBBY: What!

SHERIFF: No, we've altered the rules since you left us, and now anyone can join the force.

ROBBY: Aw, great! And can I have a star, Dad?

SHERIFF: You can have both a star and a gun, son. Here you are. *(He gives ROBBY a spare gun and a star. Applause)*.

ROBBY: Thanks, Dad. Is it loaded?

SHERIFF: Try it.

ROBBY *shoots at the stalls. The* STALLHOLDERS *scream and duck.*

ROBBY: It's great, Dad!

SHERIFF: That's my boy! Now, who else wants to be a Deputy? Who else wants a gun and a star?

MARIAN *(stepping forward)*: I do.

All the other GIRLS *step forward one after the other, saying 'And me' and holding a hand out.*

DEPUTY 2: You! Girls can't be Deputies. It's a man's job.

BRIDGET: Robby's Dad says that anyone can join the force now. Give us the stars; we're tougher than that lot. *(Indicating the* GANG*)*

DEPUTY 2: Is this true, men? *(The* OUTLAWS *nod.)*

SHERIFF: Give them their stars.

DEPUTY 2 *presents stars to the* GIRLS *saying* 'Welcome to the force'. *Applause.*

DEPUTY 3: What about the bags of gold and silver, Sheriff?

FRIAR: Marian and the girls can share the gold to buy new
clothes. If they're going to be Deputies, they're going to have
to look smarter than they did in the forest.

DEPUTY 3: There you are, Marian. *(Applause)*

STALLHOLDER 2: What about giving us the silver? There hasn't
been much trading today with all the excitement.

SHERIFF: Fair enough. You can share it later.

The silver is handed over. Applause.

SHERIFF: I think everyone's satisfied now, and we can all go
home. *(All start to go, leaving the* GANG *huddled together
downstage.)*

STALLHOLDER 1: But what about the outlaws? What are they
going to do?

DEPUTY 3: They'll just have to go back to the forest, won't they?

MARIAN: They can't go back there, they'll starve.

WILL: Oh no we won't. We can cook as well as anybody.

ALAN: That's right. We like cooking. It's just no fun in the forest.

JOHN: No, it's miserable.

SMALLEST: And it's so cold. *(The* GANG *nod and shiver.)*

FRIAR: Well, one place where it's always warm is the castle
kitchen. There's going to be a lot of extra cooking now that
Robby's back, and there's all the new deputies to cook for.
What about it, lads, will you be the new castle cooks?

JOHN *(looking at the others)*: Do we all agree to that, lads?

OTHERS: Yes!

JOHN: Right, we'll do that, squire, er, Friar, er, Mrs Nudd.
(Laughter and applause. All line up.)

FRIAR: Good. Now everyone's satisfied.
So Robby Nudd is happy now
Back with his Ma and Pa.

SHERIFF: He's lost his band of outlaws
But he's gained a gun and a star.

GIRLS: A triumph too for Women's Lib:
      We girls have all got guns.
GANG: But it's warmer in the kitchen
      Baking tasty pies and buns.
ALL: We hope you liked our story:
      We hope we got it right.
      And now we only have to say
      Good luck, good health, good night.

CURTAIN